REMARRIAGE, POLYGAMY, AND

JESUS' TEACHING ON DIVORCE

Remarriage, Polygamy, and Jesus' Teaching on Divorce

Chastity, Adultery, and the One Flesh Union in the Old and New Testaments

May 16, 2020

Wayne ODonnell

ISBN: 9798646399916

To Cora

Jacob and Rachel by William Dyce, 1853

Gen. 29:1-29. Jacob ... came into the land of the people of the east. ... Rachel came with her father's sheep; for she kept them. ... When Jacob saw Rachel the daughter of Laban his mother's brother, ... Jacob kissed Rachel, and lifted up his voice, and wept. ... Laban had two daughters: the name of the elder was Leah, and the name of the younger was Rachel. Leah was tender eyed; but Rachel was beautiful and well favored. And Jacob loved Rachel; and said, I will serve you seven years for Rachel your younger daughter. ... And Jacob served seven years for Rachel; and they seemed unto him but a few days, for the love he had to her. And Jacob said unto Laban, "Give me my wife, for my days are fulfilled." ... And Laban gathered together all the men of the place, and made a feast. And it came to pass in the evening, that he took Leah his daughter, and brought her to him; and he went in unto her. And Laban gave unto his daughter Leah Zilpah his maid for a handmaid. And it came to pass, that in the morning, behold, it was Leah: and he said to Laban, "What's this you've done to me? Didn't I serve with you for Rachel?" ... And Laban said, "It mustn't be done so in our country, to give the younger before the firstborn. Fulfil her week, and we will give you this [Rachel] also for the service which you will serve with me yet seven other years." And Jacob did so, and fulfilled her week; and he gave him Rachel his daughter to wife also. And Laban gave to Rachel his daughter Bilhah his handmaid to be her maid.

Contents

Tables

Introduction

All my books can be read online free at WayneODonnell.com. "Freely you have received, freely give" (Mt. 10:8).

This booklet is included in and comprises a section of my book "The Special Ministries of Women: Pro-Headcovering, Pro-Remarriage in 1 Corinthians 11, Song of Solomon, and Jesus' Teaching on Divorce."

This booklet is about the one-flesh union and its implications for chastity, adultery, polygamy, divorce, and remarriage. Our modern egalitarian culture has caused people to misunderstand the Biblical definition of adultery and Jesus' teaching about divorce and remarriage; which has resulted in untold amounts of suffering over the centuries. Most modern Bible teachers let their culture determine their interpretation of the Bible, instead of letting the Bible determine their evaluation of our culture.

Men that teach divorces are invalid if they're made for invalid reasons, teach exactly the opposite of what the Bible teaches. The Bible says "She may go and be another man's wife" (Deut. 24:1-2), but they say she can't go and be another man's wife. The Bible says "to avoid fornication let every man have his own wife, and let every woman have her own husband," but they say most divorced people can't ever have a husband or wife. The Bible says, "If they can't contain, let them marry," but they say don't let them marry. The Bible says "marriage is honorable and the bed undefiled" (Heb. 13:4), but they say marriage is not honorable and undefiled for most people who remarry. The 'invalid divorce' teachers cause the same kind of harm as those that "depart from the faith, ... forbidding to marry" (1 Tim. 4:3), because they forbid the use of God's provision for avoiding fornication.

This book covers some difficult topics. I recommend considering other interpretations of the passages I dealt with, as long as they're based on the details of the text itself, and not imposed on the text by the interpreter because of his culture.

All Bible quotations are from the King James Version, but I changed the archaic parts like "thou" to "you," etc. I also replaced "Christ" with "Messiah," because both are transliterations of words meaning "anointed," and everyone knows what a "messiah" is, but not what a "christ" is, except for its mostly harmful, religious overtones.

Chastity

Women's Special Ministry of Chastity

Women have a special ministry of purity and chastity which requires virginity before marriage and faithfulness to one husband after engagement and marriage. Paul told the Corinthian church, "I am jealous over you with godly jealousy, for I have espoused you to one husband, that I may present you as a chaste virgin to Messiah," 2 Cor. 11:2. The word "chaste" here, is the Greek word "agnos," which is usually translated as "pure."

Webster's 1828 dictionary defines chastity as, "before marriage, purity from all commerce of sexes; after marriage, fidelity to the marriage bed." Faithfulness after marriage is just as chaste as virginity before marriage, because, "Marriage is honorable in all, and the bed undefiled: but whoremongers and adulterers God will judge," Heb. 13:4.

A married woman stays chaste by making love to only one man as long as he lives. "The woman which has a husband is bound by the law to her husband so long as he lives; but if the husband is dead, she is loosed from the law of her husband. So then if, while her husband lives, she is married to another man, she shall be called an adulteress: but if her husband is dead, she is free from that law; so that she is no adulteress, though she is married to another man," Rm. 7:1-2.

The Bible never says the reciprocal: "The man which has a wife is bound by the law to his wife so long as she lives; but if the wife is dead, he is loosed from the law of his wife. So then if, while his wife lives, he is married to another woman, he shall be called an adulterer: but if his wife is dead, he is free from that law; so that he is no adulterer, though he is married to another woman." The Bible doesn't treat genders symmetrically. Men also need to be pure in thought and deed, but their sexual purity is determined by how they treat the chastity of women.

Virginity Matters for Women but not Men

When Abraham sent his servant from Canaan to his relatives in Haran to find a wife for his son, Isaac, the scriptures made it very clear that Rebekah was a virgin. "Rebekah came out ... with her pitcher upon her shoulder, and the damsel was very fair to look upon, a virgin, neither had any man known her," Gen. 24:15-16. Why didn't the Bible also say Isaac was 'a virgin, neither had he known any woman?'

The same could be said regarding the "four hundred young virgins" the men of Benjamin kidnapped (Jdg. 21:12), or the "young virgin" that was found to keep King David (not a virgin) warm when he was old and had poor circulation (1 Kgs 1:2), or the "fair young virgins" gathered for King Ahasuerus (not a virgin) to choose a wife from (Est. 2:3).

In Deuteronomy 22:13-21, a man could charge his new bride with not having been a virgin. "I took this woman, and when I came to her I found she was not a virgin, then the father and mother of the young woman shall take and bring out the evidence of the young woman's virginity to the elders of the city at the gate." Why couldn't a new bride make a similar charge against her husband? "My husband later told me he wasn't a virgin when we got married." Of course, there's no "evidence of virginity" for men (and probably not dependable evidence for women either), but other people could have testified as to the groom's lack of 'virginity' if it was relevant.

There's a chapter in the Bible about a bitter water test for women suspected of adultery, but none for men. "The priest shall put her under oath, and say to the woman, 'If no man has lain with you, and if you have not gone astray to uncleanness while under your husband's authority, be free from this bitter water that brings a curse.' ... Then the priest shall write these curses in a book, and he shall scrape them off into the bitter water. And he shall make the woman drink the bitter water that brings a curse," Num. 5:17-23. This would not work today, by the way, because there's no tabernacle, temple, or priests, or indication God would honor this test in any way today.

The high priest could only marry a virgin. "He that is the high priest ... shall take a wife in her virginity; a widow, or a divorced woman, or profane, or a harlot, these shall he not take," Lev. 21:10-14. But the scripture never says of any woman, "she shall take a husband in his virginity."

In the Old Testament, the Hebrew word 'bethulah' denotes a virgin woman, whereas there's no Hebrew word to denote a 'virgin' man. For example: "Both young men, and maidens, [virgins, 'bethulah'] ... let them praise the name of the Lord," Ps. 148:12-13. "My virgins ['bethulah'] and my young men are gone into captivity, ... my virgins ['bethulah'] and my young men are fallen by the sword," Lam. 1:18;2:21. "Corn shall make the young men cheerful, and new wine the maids ['virgins', 'bethulah']," Zech. 9:17.

In the New Testament, the Greek word 'parthenos' denotes a virgin woman. "I am jealous over you with godly jealousy: for I have espoused you to one husband, that I may present you as a chaste virgin [parthenos] to Messiah," 2 Cor. 11:2. 'Parthenos' can, by extension, refer to a 'virgin' man, as it does in only one place in the Bible, in Revelation 14:4, but that's an abnormal usage.

Even traditional English, before the recent invention and popularizing of 'Ms.', differentiated between married and unmarried women by the titles 'Mrs.' and 'Miss,' but all men were just called 'Mr.' And it's only recently in our [ungodly] culture the word 'virgin' started to be used in reference to men, like in the movie, "The 40-Year-Old Virgin."

Webster's 1828 dictionary defines a virgin as, "A WOMAN who has had no carnal knowledge of man." But Webster's modern Learner's dictionary defines a virgin as "a PERSON who has not had sexual intercourse." So the definition of virgin has changed over the years, and most Bible teachers let our changing culture determine their interpretation of the Bible.

Young women start with a natural desire for chastity, but modern societies are very effective at chipping away at that mindset. David gave Solomon advice that would deliver him "from the strange woman ... which forsakes the guide of her youth, and forgets the covenant of her God, for her house inclines unto death," Prov. 2:16-18. But any woman, regardless of her past, can be chaste from any point onward by not having physical relations with any man if she's single, and by only having physical relations with her husband if she's married.

The Bible is concerned about sexual purity for both men and women; and prohibits fornication and adultery for both men and women. But men can only be chaste by not violating the chastity of any woman, and men can only be unchaste by violating the chastity of a woman. "You [married or unmarried man] shall not lie carnally with your neighbor's wife [a married woman], to defile yourself with her," Lev. 18:20. The Bible doesn't view the 'virginity' of men as relevant in getting married, because, Biblically, it's perfectly moral for the man to already have a wife when he gets married.

The Old Testament Definition of Adultery

Our modern definition of adultery is "a married person having physical relations with someone other than their spouse." But the Bible's definition of adultery is "a man having physical relations with a married or engaged woman other than his spouse." Biblically, if a man, married or unmarried, has physical relations with an unengaged and unmarried woman, he is guilty of fornication, not adultery. Biblically, only the marital status of the woman is relevant in determining adultery. Our modern definition talks about a married "person," but the biblical definition talks about a married or engaged "woman."

This is an important distinction because the biblical definition of adultery underlies everything the Bible says about marriage, divorce, and remarriage. You can't understand these things apart from the definition of adultery. Here are some examples of the Bible's definition of adultery that show that only the marital status of the woman is relevant.

"The man [married or unmarried] that commits adultery with another man's wife [a married woman], even he that commits adultery with his neighbor's wife, the adulterer and the adulteress shall surely be put to death," Lev. 20:10. The woman was married, so the sin is adultery. (Hopefully, the death penalty was probably almost never carried out, but it does indicate the seriousness of the guilt.)

"They [married or unmarried men] ... have committed adultery with their neighbors' wives [married women]," Jer. 29:23. The women were married, so the sin is adultery.

"He [married or unmarried] that goes in to his neighbor's wife [a married woman]; whoever touches her shall not be innocent; ... whoever commits adultery with a woman lacks understanding," Prov. 6:29-32. The woman was someone's wife, so the sin is adultery.

"As a wife [a married woman] that commits adultery, which takes strangers [married or unmarried] instead of her husband," Ez. 16:31-33. She's "a wife," so the sin is adultery.

"You [married or unmarried] shall not lie carnally with your neighbor's wife [a married woman], to defile yourself with her," Lev. 18:20. Neighbor's wife = married woman = adultery.

"If a man [married or unmarried] is found lying with a woman married to a husband [a married woman], then they shall both of them die," Deut. 22:22. Only the woman's marital status is relevant; the man's marital status isn't mentioned.

The Bible never says the reciprocal of any of these verses, like, "if a man married to a wife [a married man] is found lying with a woman [married or unmarried], then they shall both of them die," because the marital status of the man is always irrelevant, and the marital status of the woman is always relevant.

There are four cases in Exodus 22 and Deuteronomy 22 that also make this clear. The penalty for adultery with a married woman was death; whereas the penalty for fornication with an unmarried woman was that the man must offer to marry her.

Case 1: Seduction - Unmarried Woman - Not Adultery

"If a man [married or unmarried] entice a maid that is not betrothed [unmarried and unengaged], and lie with her, he shall surely endow her to be his wife," Ex. 22:16. It's not adultery when the woman is not engaged or married.

But the man is required to offer to marry her because he became one flesh with her. If he doesn't marry her, her chastity will be violated when she breaks her one-flesh union with him, when she later consummates her marriage to another man. However, marriage is too life-changing to be entered just because a man and woman have become one flesh. The one-flesh union is just one factor to be aware of, and to serve as a motivation to avoid fornication, because the consequences are so significant.

Case 2: Seduction - Married Woman - Adultery

"If a man [married or unmarried] is found lying with a woman married to a husband [a married woman], then they shall both of them die," Deut.

22:22. It's adultery.

Case 3: Rape - Married Woman - Adultery (with all the guilt on the man)

"If a man [married or unmarried] find a betrothed damsel [an engaged woman] in the field, and the man force her, and lie with her: then the man only that lay with her shall die, but unto the damsel you shall do nothing," Deut. 22:25-26. "Unto the damsel you shall do nothing," unlike the unimaginably cruel and ungodly practices of so-called 'honor killings' in Islam. After a gentle woman suffers such great violence from rape, instead of being helped and comforted, the false religion of Islam not only doesn't comfort her, but allows her to suffer even worse violence from those who should be helping her.

Case 4: Rape - Unmarried Woman - Not Adultery (with the guilt of the violation of chastity on the man)

"If a man [married or unmarried] find a damsel that is a virgin, which is not betrothed [unmarried and unengaged], and lay hold on her, and lie with her, and they are found; then the man that lay with her shall give unto the damsel's father fifty shekels of silver, and she shall be his wife [if she and her father so choose]," Deut. 22:28-29. Rape is horrible violence, but it's fornication, not adultery, if the woman is unmarried.

Like in the case of the seduction of an unmarried and unengaged woman, the man is required to offer to marry her because he became one flesh with her. If he doesn't marry her, her chastity will be violated when she breaks her one-flesh union with him when she later consummates her marriage to another man, but all the guilt of the violation of chastity will be put on the man that forced her. It would be unusual for such a man to be a good match, so the woman should usually refuse his offer of marriage.

The man is required to pay fifty shekels to be held by her father for her future financial security in either case. David paid 50 shekels for an area of the temple mount (2 Sam. 24:24), Jacob paid 100 pieces of money for his land in Shechem (Gen. 33:19), and Abraham paid 400 shekels for his land in Hebron (Gen. 23:16). The fifty shekels and offer to marry are probably the minimum penalty, with harsher punishment depending on the circumstances. The word for "lay hold on," "taphas," in Deut. 22:28 is less violent than the word for "force," "chazaq," in Deut. 22:25, and the phrase "and they are found" may indicate a whole range of circumstances and penalties ranging from the penalties for the seduction of a virgin in Deut. 22:22, to the death penalty for the rape of a married woman in Deut. 22:25-26.

According to Webster's 1828 dictionary, Connecticut's laws of that time gave an almost biblical definition of adultery. "The sexual intercourse of ANY man, with a MARRIED woman, is the crime of ADULTERY in both: such intercourse of a MARRIED man, with an UNMARRIED woman, is FORNICATION in both." Today's Webster's Learner's dictionary defines adultery in total contradiction to the Bible, but in harmony with our modern gender-equality culture, as "sex between a married PERSON and someone who is not that person's wife or husband."

So the definition of adultery in American society has changed from an almost biblical one back in 1828, in which only the marital status of the woman was relevant, to a totally unbiblical one today. The problem is that most Bible teachers today use society's definition of adultery to interpret the Bible without realizing they are using an unbiblical definition.

Polygamy in the Old Testament

The OT Definition of Adultery Permits Polygamy

No one can understand the biblical definition of adultery without understanding that it allows polygamy. I'm not writing about polygamy to promote it, but because modern Bible teachers have let our modern culture determine their interpretation of scripture. Every misinterpretation of scripture causes harm to people, so we need to revisit this topic regardless of the risks and difficulties. Teachers that don't understand that the biblical definition of adultery allows polygamy cannot understand Jesus' teachings about divorce and remarriage, and untold suffering has been inflicted on conscientious believers because of misinterpretations about those issues.

Since the definition of adultery only considers the marital status of the woman as relevant, then for a married man to add a second wife cannot be adultery, as long as that woman herself is unmarried and unengaged. The Bible is very concerned about whether a woman is a virgin when she marries, but considers the 'virginity' of men irrelevant, because the Bible allows a man to already be married when he marries.

Going back to the four cases that defined adultery in Exodus 22 and Deuteronomy 22, if the woman was unmarried, the act was not adultery, and the man was required to offer marriage, so the woman had the option to choose to maintain her chastity, even if the man was already married.

Case 1: Seduction - Unmarried Woman - Not Adultery

"If a man [married or unmarried] entice a maid that is not betrothed [unmarried and unengaged], and lie with her, he shall surely endow her to be his wife," Ex. 22:16, even if he's already married. The rabbis preferred an unmarried man propose to her, but married men were also required to offer marriage. "If a rumor went out concerning that she had relations with two men, ... [and] the rumor is of equal strength with regard to both, one is married and one is not married, the second has a mitzvah [obligation] to [offer to] marry her," Shulchan Aruch, Even HaEzer 117:5.

Case 4: Rape - Unmarried Woman - Not Adultery

"If a man [married or unmarried] find a damsel that is a virgin, which is not betrothed [unmarried and unengaged], and lay hold on her, and lie with her, and they are found; then the man that lay with her shall give unto the damsel's father fifty shekels of silver, and she shall be his wife [if she and her father so choose]," Deut. 22:28-29, even if the man is already married. The rabbis said, "One who rapes a virgin must marry her, as long as she and her father so desire. ... And he may never divorce her except with her consent," Shulchan Aruch, Even HaEzer 117:3.

Rape is a horrible and often violent sin, but it's not 'adultery' if the woman is not married, and so the man is required to offer to marry her, and no exception is made for if he's already married. The woman is totally innocent, even if she refuses his offer, which is almost always the best choice, and the violation of her chastity when she marries someone else later will be laid to the account of the man that forced her. Usually, a rapist is only suited for jail, not marriage; but there are possible exceptions, like Shechem and Amnon.

Before Moses gave the law, "Dinah the daughter of Leah, which she bare unto Jacob, went out to see the daughters of the land. When Shechem the son of Hamor the Hivite, prince of the country, saw her, he took her, and lay with her, and defiled her. And his soul clave unto Dinah the daughter of Jacob, and he loved the damsel, and spoke kindly unto the damsel. And Shechem spoke unto his father Hamor, saying, Get me this damsel to wife," Gen. 34:1-4. But Dinah's brothers, Simeon and Levi, didn't ask Dinah what she thought. They killed Shechem, and all the men of his city, and added their wives and children to their own.

And after Moses gave the law, much trouble may have been avoided if the requirement for a rapist to offer marriage had been followed in the case of Amnon. "Absalom the son of David had a fair sister, whose name was Tamar; and Amnon the son of David loved her. And Amnon was so vexed, that he fell sick for his [half] sister Tamar," and was "lean from day to day," 2 Sam. 13:1-2. He eventually forced her and as soon as his lust was satisfied, he hated her, and "said unto her, Arise, be gone. And she said unto him, 'There is no cause. This evil in sending me away is greater than the other that you did unto me.' ... When king David heard of all these things, he was very wroth," 1 Sam. 13:15-21. But Amnon was never required to offer to marry her; and Absalom, Tamar's brother, eventually killed Amnon, which led to a civil war that almost took David's life also.

God also commanded Jewish men to offer to marry their brother's wife if their brother died without children, even if they themselves were already married. Would God ever have commanded a married man to marry an additional wife if it were adultery?

"If brethren dwell together, and one of them die, and have no child, the wife of the dead [now unmarried] shall not marry without unto a stranger: her husband's brother [married or unmarried] shall go in unto her, and take her to him to wife, and perform the duty of a husband's brother unto her. And it shall be, that the firstborn which she bears shall succeed in the name of his brother which is dead, that his name be not put out of Israel," Deut. 25:5.

The surviving brothers were not forced to marry the widow, but the eldest was shamed by a "Release," or "Chalitza" ceremony if none of them did. "Then the elders of his city shall call him, and speak unto him: and if he stand to it, and say, I like not to take her; then shall his brother's wife come unto him in the presence of the elders, and loose his shoe from off his foot, and spit in his face, and shall answer and say, 'So shall it be done unto that man that will not build up his brother's house.' And his name shall be called in Israel, 'The house of him that hath his shoe loosed,'" Deut. 25:8-10.

The Jewish rabbis recognized a man can't marry his brother's widow if he's already married to her sister, for example. "You shall not uncover the nakedness of a woman and her daughter. ... Neither shall you take a wife with her sister, to vex her, to uncover her nakedness, beside the other in her life time," Lev. 18:17-18. But just already being married isn't a valid excuse.

"Someone who has many wives, and dies, and has a brother, the intercourse or Release of one of them removes the obligations of the others, and the brother can only marry one of them. ... One [brother] marries or releases one of the wives and [this act] allows the rest of them [to marry someone else]. The [primacy of] commandment is on the eldest brother to marry ... or release. If he doesn't want, ... or he can't free her or marry her, e.g. he's married to her sister ... [the commandment] returns to each brother in the order of their age. If none of them want, we return to the eldest and say to him; the commandment is yours, either Release her or marry her. If he doesn't want to ... marry or Release her, we force him to Release her, but we don't force him to marry her. ... In our times, Chalitza is given priority." Shulchan Aruch, Even HaEzer 161:4.

I don't believe rabbinic writings are authoritative. In fact, the rabbis of Jesus generation didn't reject him for offering a spiritual kingdom, since he actually offered a physical Messianic Kingdom just like they were expecting; but they rejected him because he rejected their "oral law" they claimed their ancestors had received at Mt. Sinai from Moses, on the side, as it were (Mt. 12:1-14). But I reference rabbinic texts because the rabbis have put a lot of thought and discussion into these issues, since they actually had to apply them as law, though their ability to apply them was limited while they were outside the land since 132 AD.

David's life also shows that the biblical definition of adultery allows polygamy. When David was young he married Michal, Saul's daughter. Later, while fleeing from Saul, David married two more single women, Ahinoam, and the virtuous Abigail (1 Sam. 25). God didn't rebuke David for marrying the single women Ahinoam and Abigail while he was already married to Michal. But when David committed adultery with Bathsheba, a married woman, God rebuked him through Nathan the prophet, and punished him for an extended period of time.

"Nathan said to David, ... thus says the Lord God of Israel, I anointed you king over Israel, ... and I gave you ... your master's wives into your bosom, ... and if that had been too little, I would moreover have given unto you such and such things. ... Now therefore the sword shall never depart from your house. Because you have ... taken the wife of Uriah the Hittite to be your wife, ... I will take your wives before your eyes, and give them unto your neighbor, and he shall lie with your wives in the sight of this sun. ... And the Lord struck the child that Uriah's wife bare unto David, and it was very sick," 2 Sam. 12:7-24.

Notice that Bathsheba was not referred to by name in this part of the passage, but as "the wife of Uriah," and "Uriah's wife," because it was her marital status that made David's action sinful, not his marital status in already having several wives. "Because you have ... taken the wife of Uriah the Hittite to be your wife, ... the Lord struck the child that Uriah's wife bare unto David," 2 Sam. 12:10,15. However, from that point on, she's referred to by name in the passage, and the marriage was legitimate, though what led to it was not. "And David comforted Bathsheba his wife, and went in unto her, and lay with her: and she bare a son, and he called his name Solomon [the future king]: and the Lord loved him," 2 Sam. 12:24.

Thus, a man having physical relations with the wife of another man, like Uriah's, is adultery; but being married to multiple wives is not adultery. Notice also that back in verse 8, God told David he "gave you ... your master's wives [plural] into your bosom." God wouldn't have given David multiple wives if polygamy was in any way sinful.

At least one Bible scholar had enough respect for God's word to change his opinion from the current, popular one to the biblical one. The Rev. William F. Luck, Sr., is a former Professor of Moody Bible Institute. He's published numerous articles in Moody Monthly, Christianity Today, the Southern Presbyterian Journal, and the Journal of the Evangelical Theological Society.

In the 2nd edition of his book, "Divorce and Remarriage; Recovering the Biblical View," he says "In ... writing a book on marriage, divorce and remarriage in the Bible, I was motivated by the fact that God didn't ask me my opinion about the issue. He expected me to represent His. I've tried. If you can prove I'm mistaken, I'll be the first to thank you. But I'm not holding my breath in the meanwhile. It never crossed my mind, when I started my research on the book, that the Old Testament law allowed polygyny. Of course I knew that some people in ancient times practiced it, but I thought it was a sin, perhaps one that God winked at. My first clue that I was mistaken came when I attempted to define "adultery" from a biblical perspective. I had no doubt in my mind that "adultery" would be defined as "any sexual relationship between a married person and someone other than their spouse." I could not even imagine another definition. So imagine my surprise when I sought, like a good little

Evangelical fundamentalist, to find verses which "proved up" that (working) definition, and found instead that adultery was always defined by the woman's marital status, never the man's."

When I use the term "polygamy" in this chapter, I'm actually referring only to "polygyny," the form of polygamy where a man marries more than one woman. "Polyandry," the form of polygamy where a woman marries more than one man, is obviously strictly forbidden by the Bible's definition of adultery.

Many Bible teachers today will say polygamy was never right, but that God overlooked it in the lives of a few men in the Old Testament, the same way he overlooked other sins in their lives, like murder. But 1) God explicitly forbade things like murder and sodomy while he never explicitly forbade polygamy; 2) it's not true that God overlooked sins like adultery and murder as we saw in the example of David; and 3) the Bible doesn't present God as merely overlooking the polygamy of a few people, but as going out of his way to use polygamists as some of his greatest servants from the time of Abraham onward. God even portrays himself as a polygamist.

God Portrays Himself as a Polygamist

Samaria was the capital of the northern kingdom of Israel, and Jerusalem was the capital of the southern kingdom of Judah. God was married to both of them at the same time. They both committed adultery, so God allowed them both to be carried away into captivity into the lands of their lovers. First Israel was carried to Assyria, and then Judah was carried into Babylon.

Ezekiel 23, "Son of man, there were two women. ... They were mine, and they bore sons and daughters. As for their names, Samaria is Oholah, and Jerusalem is Oholibah. ... Oholah [Samaria] played the harlot even though she was mine; and she lusted for her lovers, the neighboring Assyrians; ... with all their idols, she defiled herself. ... Therefore I have delivered her into the hand of her lovers, into the hand of the Assyrians, for whom she lusted. ... Now although her sister Oholibah [Jerusalem] saw this, she became more corrupt in her lust than she, and in her harlotry more corrupt than her sister's harlotry. ... The Babylonians came to her, into the bed of love. ... Then I alienated myself from her, as I had alienated myself from her sister."

God tells the same story in Jeremiah 2 and 3. "Of Jerusalem, ... thus says the Lord. I remember you, the kindness of your youth, the love of your betrothal, when you went after me in the wilderness. ... Have you seen what backsliding Israel [the northern kingdom] has done? She has gone up on every high mountain and under every green tree, and there played the harlot. And I said, after she had done all these things, 'Return to Me,' but she did not return. And her treacherous sister Judah [the southern kingdom] saw it. Then I saw that for all the causes for which backsliding Israel had committed adultery, I had put her away and given her a certificate of divorce; yet her treacherous sister Judah did not fear, but went and played the harlot also. ... Return, O backsliding children, says the Lord; for I am married to you."

God divorced the northern kingdom of Israel. Once they were taken into captivity by Assyria they never returned to Canaan as a nation, though some individuals from the northern kingdom undoubtedly returned and their descendants will someday be gathered back. God didn't divorce the southern kingdom of Judah, but only separated from her. After seventy years in Babylon, many captives returned together to reestablish the kingdom of Judah. Whereas God says he gave the northern kingdom a writ of divorce, "I had put her away and given her a certificate of divorce," Jer. 3:8; he says he never gave the southern kingdom one, "Thus says the

Lord, 'Where is the bill of your mother's divorcement, whom I have put away?'" Is. 50:1.

And God tells the same story in Ezekiel 16. Notice the story will eventually have a happy ending. "Thus says the Lord God to Jerusalem. ... When I passed by you again and looked upon you, indeed your time was the time of love. ... I swore an oath to you and entered into a covenant with you, and you became mine, says the Lord God. ... But you trusted in your own beauty, played the harlot because of your fame. ... Behold, therefore, I ... will judge you as women who break wedlock ... are judged. ... Your elder sister is Samaria, who dwells with her daughters to the north of you. ... You did not walk in their ways nor act according to their abominations; but, as if that were too little, you became more corrupt than they in all your ways. ... I will deal with you as you have done, who despised the oath by breaking the covenant. Nevertheless I will remember My covenant with you in the days of your youth, and I will establish an everlasting covenant with you."

Would the eternal, unchangeable God ever portray himself as being married to more than one woman at the same time if polygamy was, is, or ever will be sinful in any way? God would never portray himself as an adulterer or a homosexual (God forbid), and he would never portray himself as a polygamist if there was anything immoral about it.

By the time of the Messianic Kingdom, the houses of Israel and Judah will be recombined into one nation, but even then, God will have two wives, Israel and the Church, since by then the "marriage supper of the Lamb," Rev. 19:9, will have taken place. Some say God the Father is married to Israel, and Jesus Messiah will be married to the church, but God is one. God will be married to a reunited Israel and Judah and also to the church. So God has and always will portray himself as a polygamist, and therefore polygamy can't be wrong. "Is there unrighteousness with God? God forbid!" Rm. 9:14. "Let God be true, but every man a liar," Rm. 3:4.

God Chose a Polygamist to Write His Marriage Manual

Solomon sinned by marrying too many wives. He had 1000 wives and concubines, and God had said the kings of Israel "shall not multiply horses to himself, ... neither shall he multiply wives to himself, that his heart turn not away: neither shall he greatly multiply to himself silver and gold," Deut. 17:16-17. Now this didn't mean Solomon wasn't allowed to have more than one wife, any more than it meant he wasn't allowed to have more than one horse, or more than one piece of silver or gold. He was permitted to 'add wives to himself', but he was not permitted to "multiply wives to himself," Deut. 17:17. He was permitted more than one, but not a great many.

And though Solomon was the wisest man that ever lived, he took so many foreign wives for political alliances that they led him into idolatry, which resulted in his kingdom being split into Israel and Judah. "King Solomon surpassed all the kings of the earth in riches and wisdom. ... But King Solomon loved many foreign women, as well as the daughter of Pharaoh, women of the Moabites, Ammonites, Edomites, Sidonians, and Hittites. ... Solomon clung to these in love. And he had seven hundred wives, princesses, and three hundred concubines. And ... it was so, when Solomon was old, that his wives turned his heart after other gods. ... The Lord said to Solomon, 'Because you have done this, ... I will surely tear the kingdom away from you and give it to your servant. ... However, ... I will give one tribe [Judah] to your son for the sake of My servant David, and for the sake of Jerusalem which I have chosen.'" 1 Kgs. 10:23-11:13.

But despite the fact that Solomon sinned by "multiplying" wives, God chose him, the most extreme polygamist in the Bible, possibly in history, to write the Bible's marriage manual. It's called the Song of Songs, and it's the love story of Solomon and his one hundred and fortieth wife, Shulamith. We know more about the romance, wedding, and married life of Shulamith than of any other woman in the Bible because Solomon wrote the book from her perspective, often narrating even her own thoughts by divine revelation.

(As the book begins we share in Shulamith's nervousness the first time that she, a poor country girl, was brought to the palace and presented to the women of the court.)

[Shulamith's narration]
"The king has brought me into his chambers," Song 1:4.

[Shulamith to the women of the court]
"I *am* dark, but lovely,
O daughters of Jerusalem,
Like the tents of Kedar,
Like the curtains of Solomon.
Do not look upon me, because I *am* dark,
Because the sun has tanned me," Song 1:5-6.

(Solomon publicly expressed his support for her and thus won over the women of the court to her.)

[Solomon]
"I have compared you, my love,
To my filly among Pharaoh's chariots.
Your cheeks are lovely with ornaments,
Your neck with chains of gold," Song 1:9-10.

[Women of the court to Shulamith]
"We will make you ornaments of gold
With studs of silver," Song 1:11.

(Shulamith liked Solomon because of his good character and reputation.)

[Shulamith]
"Your name is as ointment poured forth," Song 1:3.

(And she liked his gentleness and appreciation of beauty.)

[Shulamith]
"He feeds his flock among the lilies," Song 4:16.

(Solomon cared for, protected, and provided for Shulamith. He was a safe haven for her; a place free of criticism.)

[Shulamith]
"Like an apple tree among the [non-fruit] trees of the woods, so is my beloved among the sons. I

sat down in his shade with great delight," Song
2:3.

(We learn about their outings to the countryside,
their wedding day, the details of their wedding
night, and some of their arguments and making
up afterwards. And we are admonished over and
over in the book not to arouse passion by
physical contact before marriage.)

[Shulamith]
"I charge you, O daughters of Jerusalem,
By the gazelles or by the doe of the field,
Do not stir up nor awaken love
Until it pleases," Song 4:7.

(We even get to meet her brothers who helped
protect her chastity after their father died. If she
was too shy, they would help her meet people;
and if she was too open, they would chase away
undesirable suitors.)

[Shulamith's Brothers]
"We have a little sister,
And she has no breasts.
What shall we do for our sister
In the day when she is spoken for?
If she is a wall,
We will build upon her
A battlement of silver;

And if she is a door,
We will enclose her
With boards of cedar," Song 8:8-9.

Why would God have chosen the most extreme polygamist in the Bible to write the Bible's marriage manual if polygamy was in any way sinful? Couldn't he have found a single monogamist in all the years from Moses to Solomon to write it instead? Wouldn't he be sending the wrong message about marriage by using a polygamous marriage as the Bible's model marriage if polygamy is ever wrong?

Every Book in the Bible About Women Is About Polygamists

There are three books in the Old Testament that focus on a woman: The Book of Ruth, the Song of Solomon, and the Book of Esther. All three are about polygamists. Ruth was a Moabitess who married one of Naomi's sons when she and her husband moved to Moab to escape a famine in Israel. Naomi's husband and sons died in Moab, and so she told her daughters-in-law to stay in Moab, while she returned to Bethlehem. But Ruth said the famous words, "Where you go, I will go; and where you lodge, I will lodge. Your people shall be my people, and your God my God. Where you die, will I die, and there will I be buried," Ruth 1:16-17.

After they arrived in Bethlehem, Ruth went out to glean the harvest leftovers, as the poor were allowed to do under the law, and by God's grace she chose to glean in the field of Boaz, a near kinsman of her deceased husband, who was willing to perform the duty of a kinsman redeemer, and marry her. Though we don't know for sure, Boaz probably already had a wife when he married Ruth, because he was old, wealthy, and a ruler in the tribe of Judah; and there was no allowance in scripture for a man to avoid becoming a kinsman redeemer because he was already married.

The Book of Esther is also about polygamists. Esther, a beautiful and humble orphan of the captives in Persia, was raised by her uncle Mordecai, and competed with other maidens to become Queen of Persia. Esther was chosen as queen without revealing she was Jewish, and then the enemy Haman convinced the king to kill all Jewish people in the empire. Mordecai asked Esther to try to intervene on behalf of her people, and though the queen of an empire, she continued to obey her foster father, Mordecai.

We hear Esther issue her famous statement, "I go in unto the king, which is not according to the law;

and if I perish, I perish," Est. 4:16. Then we hold our breath with her as she enters unsummoned into the king's presence, the penalty of which is death, unless the king raises the golden scepter. "When the king saw Esther the queen standing in the court, ... she obtained favor in his sight: and the king held out to Esther the golden scepter that was in his hand. So Esther drew near, and touched the top of the scepter," Est. 5:2. And we already saw that the Song of Solomon is about polygamists. So all the books in the Old Testament about women are about polygamist women.

Another romantic love story in the Bible is that of Jacob and Rachel. "Jacob went on his journey, and came into the land of the people of the east. ... And ... Rachel came with her father's sheep; for she kept them. And it came to pass, when Jacob saw Rachel the daughter of Laban his mother's brother, ... Jacob kissed Rachel, and lifted up his voice, and wept. ... And Jacob loved Rachel; and said [to her father], I will serve you seven years for Rachel your younger daughter. ... And Jacob served seven years for Rachel; and they seemed unto him but a few days, for the love he had to her," Gen. 29:1-20. Most women would love to be loved like that. And Jacob continued to love Rachel like that, though he also had three other wives.

Most of the Bible Was Written By and About Polygamists

Moses, the law giver, was a polygamist. He married both Zipporah, who was the daughter of Jethro the Kenite/Midianite (Ex. 2:21; Ex. 3:1; Ex. 18:6; Jdg. 4:11); and he also married an Ethiopian woman (Num. 12:1). Moses wrote the Torah, the Law of God, the first five books of the Bible, and the very beginning of scriptural revelation.

The following nine books of the Bible were written by known polygamists: Moses wrote Genesis, Exodus, Leviticus, Numbers, and Deuteronomy. David wrote Psalms. Solomon wrote Proverbs, Ecclesiastes, and Song of Solomon.

1st and 2nd Samuel were written by a man from a polygamist family. "Elkanah ... had two wives; the name of the one was Hannah, ... {who] bare a son, and called his name Samuel," 1 Sam. 1:1-20. And as we saw earlier Jeremiah and Ezekiel both portray God as a polygamist. We saw that Ruth and Esther are about polygamists, and most of 1st and 2nd Kings and 1st and 2nd Chronicles are about polygamist kings.

Thus almost two-thirds of the pages of the Bible, including the New Testament, were written by or about polygamists. Was God really so short of monogamists that he had to use polygamists to write most of the Bible if monogamy is the only godly form of marriage?

We don't really know how many men in the Bible were polygamists, because the Bible doesn't usually include the names of men's wives in genealogies. Therefore, it's impossible to prove that men we might assume were monogamists had only one wife. Polygamy must have been very widespread beyond those specifically named because of all the women taken in war, for example.

In Genesis, "the sons of Jacob ... spoiled the city, ... and their wives took they captive," Gen. 34:27-29. The Law of Moses says, "when you go forth to war against your enemies, ... and see among the captives a beautiful woman, and have a desire unto her, that you would have her to your wife, then you shall bring her home to your house," Deut. 21:10-11. When Israel defeated the Midianites, "the booty ... which the men of war had caught, was ... thirty and two thousand ... women that had not known man by lying with him," Num. 31:32-35. The prophetess Deborah sang, "have they not divided the prey; to every man a damsel or two," Jdg. 5:30. In the tribe of Issachar , "the sons of Uzzi, ... five, all of them chief men. And with them, by their generations, ...

six and thirty thousand men: for they had many wives and sons," 1 Chr. 7:3-4.

Some Bible teachers admit there were a few heroes of faith that were polygamists, but that God overlooked their polygamy, and used them anyway. But that's not the way the Bible presents it. It was the greatest men of faith that were polygamists. Who are greater heroes of faith and obedience than Abraham, Jacob, Moses, and David? Abraham was called, "the friend of God," James 2:23; Jacob's name was changed to "Israel" since all his descendants comprise the Jewish people, Gen. 32:28; Moses wrote the Law, the measure of righteousness; and David was called "a man after God's own heart," Acts 13:22. And other less known heroes, like Caleb and Gideon, were polygamists too.

All Jewish people are physical descendants of the polygamist Jacob; and all Gentile believers are spiritual descendants of the polygamist Abraham. "It is of faith, ... to the end the promise might be sure to all the seed, ... which is of the faith of Abraham, who is the father of us all," Rm. 4:16. "If you are Messiah's, then are you Abraham's seed, and heirs according to the promise," Gal. 3:29.

We know these men of God did not commit fornication or adultery by marrying more than one wife, because Paul says, "neither fornicators, nor idolaters, nor adulterers, nor homosexuals ... will inherit the kingdom," 1 Cor. 6:9. Yet we know the polygamist David will be in the kingdom. "They shall serve ... David their king, whom I will raise up [resurrect] unto them," Jer. 30:9. Jesus will be "King of Kings," Rev. 19:16, and under him will be kings of individual countries, like David over Israel. We know the polygamists Abraham and Jacob will be in the kingdom, because Jesus said, "many shall come from the east and west, and shall sit down with Abraham, and Isaac, and Jacob in the kingdom," Mt. 8:11. None of these polygamists lived adulterous lives, or they couldn't inherit the kingdom. "[No] adulterers ... will inherit the kingdom," 1 Cor. 6:9.

There were polygamists in the early church. The entire church was comprised only of believing Jews and Jewish proselytes until Acts 15; and even after that time Paul always preached, "to the Jew first," Rm. 1:16. In 393 AD, the Roman emperor Theodosius prohibited Jewish men from practicing polygamy; but it wasn't until about 1000 AD that a rabbi (Gershom) prohibited it.

In Timothy and Titus, Paul says "A pastor then must be blameless, the husband of one wife, ... one that rules well his own house," 1 Tim. 3:2-6. And "For this cause left I you in Crete, that you should ... ordain elders in every city. ... If any is blameless, the husband of one wife, having faithful children," Titus. 1:6. The phrase, "husband of one wife" was probably meant to exclude polygamists in the churches from being pastors, because though polygamy was permitted, it was not ideal, and a man with more than one wife had enough to do already. In contrast, only widows "having been the wife of one husband," 1 Tim. 5:9, meaning they had been married only once, were financially supported by the churches.

I don't think the phrase "husband of one wife" can mean "a one-woman man" as many modern teachers interpret it, because that sounds like a modern phrase, and the context is about ruling one's family well. It's about 'husbands' and 'wives', not 'men' and 'women.'

The tragedy is, that not only would great men of God like Abraham, Jacob, Moses, and David not be allowed to be pastors in churches today; their families wouldn't even be allowed to attend, because modern churches would excommunicate them as adulterers, in opposition to the Bible and God's love of his precious children.

God will never let us put polygamy out of our minds. Today, every Jewish person is descended from one of Jacob's four wives; and via genetic testing or future revelation, they will eventually know which of his four wives they are descended from. In the future, when you visit Israel during the Messianic Kingdom, you'll be reminded that the polygamist David will be head of Israel's government during that time.

Also, every time you enter or leave the future world capital of Jerusalem during the Messianic Kingdom, you will be reminded of Jacob's four wives, because the the names of gates will be arranged in order of the moms of the twelve tribes. "The gates of the city shall be named after the tribes of Israel, the three gates northward [for Leah's sons]: one gate for Reuben, one gate for Judah, and one gate for Levi; on the east side ... three gates [for Rachel and Bilhah's sons]: one gate for Joseph, one gate for Benjamin, and one gate for Dan; on the south side ... three gates [for Leah's sons]: one gate for Simeon, one gate for Issachar, and one gate for Zebulun; on the west side ... three gates [for Zilpah and Bilhah's sons]: one gate for Gad, one gate for Asher, and one gate for Naphtali. ... And the name of the city from that day shall be The Lord is There," Ez. 48:30-35.

And for eternity, their names will also be on the gates of the New Jerusalem that will descend out of heaven from God. "He ... showed me that great city, the holy Jerusalem, descending out of heaven from God, having the glory of God, ... and had twelve gates, and at the gates twelve angels, and names written thereon, which are the names of the twelve tribes of the children of Israel," Rev. 21:10-12.

God Never Forbade Polygamy & Sometimes Commanded It

Nowhere in the Bible is polygamy explicitly forbidden or condemned. Don't you think there's been enough confusion about polygamy in the world throughout the ages for God to have explicitly forbidden it at least once if it was immoral? Wasn't there enough space in the Bible? In the 78 verses of Numbers 7:10-88, God repeats twelve times that each prince offered, "one silver charger, ... one silver bowl, ... one spoon," etc. Couldn't he have replaced just one of those verses with "You shall not commit polygamy," or "You shall not have more than one wife at a time?"

God explicitly said adultery is wrong many times, like in the seventh of the ten commandments, "You shall not commit adultery," Ex. 20:14. And, "The man who commits adultery with another man's wife ... shall surely be put to death," Lev. 20:10. And, "You shall not commit adultery," Deut. 5:18.

God explicitly said homosexuality is wrong many times, like in, "You shall not lie with a male as with a woman. It is an abomination," Lev. 18:22. And, "Their women exchanged the natural use for what is against nature. Likewise also the men, leaving the natural use of the woman, burned in their lust for one another, men with men committing what is shameful," Rm. 1:26-27.

And God couldn't bother to say polygamy is wrong even once? Why couldn't he just add two words about polygamy to the list of sins in 1 Corinthians 6:9-10, "Do not be deceived; neither fornicators, nor idolaters, nor adulterers, nor effeminate, nor homosexuals, [why not, 'nor polygamists'] ... will inherit the kingdom of God."

By the way, the reason you won't find the word 'polygamy' anywhere in the Bible is because the Bible simply calls it 'marriage,' regardless of the number of wives. We know the Bible doesn't call it 'adultery,' as we saw from the definition of adultery in the Bible.

Instead of being explicitly prohibited, polygamy is sometimes explicitly commanded by God. We saw that a man who seduced or raped an unmarried and unengaged woman was required to offer to marry her, even if he was already married. And we saw that God commanded Jewish men to offer to marry their brother's wife, if their brother died without children, even if they themselves were already married.

Instead of prohibiting polygamy in the Bible, God regulates it, along with other regulations about marriage. He says if a married man "take him another wife; her [the first wife's] food, her raiment, and her duty of marriage [physical love], shall he not diminish," Ex. 21:10. [I'm sure Solomon failed at that last item.] Also, "if a man have two wives, one beloved, and another hated, ... he may not make the son of the beloved firstborn before the son of the hated, which is indeed the firstborn, but he shall acknowledge the son of the hated for the firstborn, by giving him a double portion of all that he has," Deut. 21:15-17. These verses teach that a man must continue to be a good husband to his first wife, even if he marries a second.

So if it's a sin to fail to continue to be a good husband to a first wife after taking a second, then it's a far greater sin to divorce, and not be a husband at all to a first wife, and then take a second. But that's exactly what the laws of our ungodly, secular society require men to do. Our modern laws allow a man to live with as many women as he wants, simultaneously or sequentially, just so long as he doesn't commit by marriage to caring and providing for them, because as soon as he does that, it's considered bigamy. Modern law promotes 'serial polygamy,' where a man divorces and remarries one woman after another; but God's law promotes the chastity of women, and an unending commitment to protect and provide for them.

Polygamy in the New Testament

The Definition of Adultery Can't Change from Age to Age

There are three kinds of things in the world: moral, immoral, and amoral. Things that are inherently moral or immoral, are eternal and can't change from age to age or place to place. Only things that are amoral, not inherently right or wrong in themselves, can change. These amoral things become moral when God commands them, because it's always moral to do what God commands; and they become immoral when God forbids them, because it's always immoral to do what God forbids.

Dietary laws are an example of amoral things, that became moral or immoral, depending on God's commands for any particular people at any particular time. Adam was only allowed to eat plants, "I have given every green herb for meat," Gen. 1:30. Noah was allowed to eat anything that moved, "every moving thing that lives shall be meat for you," Gen. 9:3. Moses was not allowed to eat pork, "the swine, though he divides the hoof, and is cloven-footed, yet he chews not the cud; he is unclean to you," Lev. 11:7. And the church is not allowed to eat blood, "write unto them, that they abstain from pollutions of idols, and from fornication, and from things strangled, and from blood," Acts 15:20.

Dietary laws can change from age to age, because food is not inherently moral or immoral. Jesus said, "Not what goes into the mouth defiles a man; but what comes out of the mouth, this defiles a man. ... Whatever enters the mouth goes into the stomach and is eliminated, but those things which proceed out of the mouth come from the heart, and they defile a man. For out of the heart proceed evil thoughts, murders, adulteries, fornications, thefts, false witness, blasphemies. These are the things which defile a man," Mt. 15:11-20. "Adultery" is not an amoral thing, but an immoral thing, and so its definition can't change from age to age.

The NT Continues the OT Definition of Adultery

The Old Testament says a woman can only be married to one man at a time, because a woman's husband has to divorce her or die, for her to be able to marry another man. "Let him write her a bill of divorcement, and ... she may go and be another man's wife. And if the latter husband ... write her a bill of divorcement, ... or if the latter husband die ... ," Deut. 24:1-4.

But the Bible never says the reciprocal, that a man can only be married to one woman at a time, because a man's wife has to divorce him or die, for him to be able to marry another woman. It never says anything like the reciprocal of Deuteronomy 24:1-4, "let him write her a bill of divorcement, and ... he may take another wife. And if he ... write his latter wife a bill of divorcement, ... or if the latter wife die ... ."

The Old Testament also says remarriage defiles a divorced woman in regards to a previous husband. "If the latter husband die, ... her former husband, which sent her away, may not take her again to be his wife, after that she is defiled," Deut. 24:1-4. But the Bible never says the reciprocal, that remarriage defiles a divorced man, like "if the latter wife die, ... his former wife, which he sent away, may not become his wife again, after that he is defiled," because men can't be defiled by having more than one wife, either at the same time or sequentially. A divorced man can marry any number of wives, and he's still able to remarry a former wife; so long as she herself hasn't remarried, which would defile her to him.

The New Testament continues to uphold the difference between men and women in regards to chastity. Romans 7:2-3 says, "The woman which has a husband is bound by the law to her husband so long as he lives, ... so then if, while her husband lives, she is married to another man, she shall be called an adulteress." But the New Testament never says the reciprocal, like "the man which has a wife is bound by the law to his wife so long as she lives, ... so then if, while his wife lives, he is married to another woman, he shall be called an adulterer." The New Testament requires a wife to be one flesh with only one husband as long as he lives, but it doesn't require a husband to be one flesh with only one wife as long as she lives.

1 Corinthians 7:39 says the same thing. "The wife is bound by the law as long as her husband lives; but if her husband is dead, she is at liberty to be married to whom she will; only in the Lord." The New Testament never says the reciprocal, like "the husband is bound by the law as long as his wife lives; but if his wife is dead, he is at liberty to be married to whom he will; only in the Lord." A husband is already "at liberty to be married to whom he will" even while still married to his current wife, even in New Testament times.

In the passages on divorce in the gospels, Jesus

said a man who marries a divorced woman always commits adultery, because by marrying her he breaks her one-flesh union with her x-husband (or with some other man if there was another in between). But Jesus never said a woman who marries a divorced man commits adultery.

Mt. 5:32, "Whoever shall marry her that is divorced commits adultery," but never, "whoever shall marry him that is divorced commits adultery."

Mt. 19:9, "Whoever marries her which is put away commits adultery," but never "whoever marries him who put her away commits adultery."

Lu. 16:18, "Whoever marries her that is put away from her husband commits adultery," but never, "whoever marries him that put away his wife from him commits adultery."

Jesus also mentions an exception clause "saving for the cause of fornication," Mt. 5:32, and "except it be for fornication," Mt. 19:9, for when a husband divorces a wife; but never for when a wife divorces her husband. "If a woman shall put away her husband, and be married to another, she commits adultery [no exception clause for her husband having committed fornication]," Mk. 10:12. Remarriage is always a violation of the one-flesh union for women, regardless of the circumstances (though the x-husband usually bears the guilt of her remarriage if he divorced her.)

There's no need for an exception clause to determine which party is guilty of adultery when a wife divorces her husband, because a wife can't "cause" her husband to commit adultery by divorcing him, because men are permitted to be one flesh with more than one woman at a time, so long as the women themselves aren't married to someone else.

A husband who divorces an innocent wife "causes her to commit adultery," Mt. 5:32, but the Bible never says the reciprocal that a wife who divorces an innocent husband "causes him to commit adultery." A husband can only commit adultery by sinning against the chastity of his own wife, by divorcing her; or by sinning against the chastity of another man's wife, by having physical relations with her. His own marital status is irrelevant.

In 1 Corinthians 7:2, Paul was very careful to use an entirely different Greek word for "own" when he said, "To avoid fornication, let every man have his own ['heautou'] wife, and let every woman have her own ['idios'] husband." When Paul said "his own wife," he used 'heautou,' which means 'one's own reflexively and exclusively,' as in: "his own [heautou] life," Lu. 14:26; "his own [heautou] body," Rm. 4:19; "their own [heautou] dead," Gal. 6:4. A person's life and body are his exclusively, a family's dead relatives are theirs exclusively, and every wife a man has is his exclusively.

But when Paul said "her own husband," he used the Greek word 'idios' which means 'the one that pertains to you but can pertain to others also,' as in: "his own [idios] generation," Acts 13:36; "his own [idios] country," Jn. 4:44; "his own [idios] language," Acts 2:6, "his own [idios] master," Rm. 14:4. Only one generation, homeland, native language, and master pertains to each person; but it's appropriate for that generation, homeland, native language, and master to pertain to others also, as one husband can pertain to more than one wife.

For example, Sarah had her "own" husband, who was also Hagar's own husband. "After this manner in the old time the holy women also, who trusted in God, adorned themselves, being in subjection unto their own [idios] husbands; even as Sara obeyed Abraham, calling him lord," 1 Pet. 3:5-6, as Hagar did also.

In 1 Corinthians 7:10-11, Paul said to wives, "Let not the wife depart from her husband," and then he added, "but and if she depart, let her <u>remain</u>

unmarried or be reconciled to her husband." Of husbands, Paul said "and let not the husband put away his wife," but he didn't add, like he did for the wife, "but and if he put away his wife, let him remain unmarried or be reconciled to his wife." For one thing, a husband might not be unmarried after divorce. He may already be married to more than one wife at the time of the divorce, even in the New Testament; whereas a wife will always be "unmarried" after divorce.

Hebrews 13:4 says, "Marriage is honorable in all, and the bed undefiled; but whoremongers and adulterers God will judge." Whoremongers are men [married or unmarried] who commit fornication with unmarried women; and adulterers are men [married or unmarried] who commit adultery with married women. The marital statuses of the men aren't mentioned, because they aren't relevant for determining adultery in the NT as well as in the OT.

The definition of adultery permitted polygamy in the Old Testament, and these verses show that the New Testament continues the Old Testament definition of adultery, and so also continues to permit polygamy.

Jesus' Teaching on Divorce and Remarriage

One Flesh

Becoming one flesh doesn't mean becoming 'one soul,' or 'one spirit,' because it says 'one flesh.' The concerns of marriage are the concerns of this physical world, which is why a single person has less distraction to serve the Lord (1 Cor. 7:35), and why there is no marriage for resurrected and glorified people (Mt. 22:30).

Becoming one flesh doesn't refer to how a child inherits DNA from both parents, because not all marriages result in children. It doesn't refer to an exchange of fluids during lovemaking, because a couple becomes one flesh even if they use condoms. It's interesting that male DNA has been found in female brains, perhaps from the men they've made love to. (I've never seen an article that says female DNA has been found in men's brains; if that could happen, men would be smarter.)

Being one flesh is a mystical union. A man and a woman become one flesh by a single act of physical lovemaking. Whether in marriage by cleaving to a 'wife', "therefore shall a man leave his father and his mother, and shall cleave [hold] to his wife: and they shall be one flesh," Gen. 2:22-24. Or outside of marriage by committing fornication, "know you not that he which is joined to a harlot is one body? For two, said he, will be one flesh," 1 Cor. 6:16. Becoming one flesh produces emotional effects and moral obligations. According to the Bible, there's no such thing as 'casual sex.'

Not only can a man and woman become one flesh, they can stop being one flesh. When Jesus said, "They are no more two, but one flesh. What God has joined together, let not man put asunder," Mt. 19:6, he was referring to the mystical one-flesh union, that should be protected via marriage.

God created women differently from men. A woman is one flesh with only the last man she made love to, whereas a man is one flesh with every woman he was the last man they made love to. This mystery is inherent in the biblical definition of adultery. "If a man [married or unmarried] entice a maid that is not betrothed, and lie with her, he shall surely endow her to become his wife," Ex. 22:16. God wouldn't command a man to offer to marry a woman if marriage with her would sunder his one-flesh union with his existing wife.

So the first time Jacob made love to Rachel, he became one flesh with Rachel. And the first time he made love to Leah, he didn't stop being one flesh with Rachel, but also became one flesh with Leah. If this were not the case, every time Jacob made love to Leah, Rachel would stop being one flesh with him even though married to him, and every time he made love to Rachel, Leah would stop being one flesh with him even though married to him, which would be utter confusion. But when Jacob's wife Bilhah made love with Reuben, she stopped being one flesh with Jacob, and became one flesh with Reuben. When Jacob made love to Bilhah again, she became one flesh with Jacob again.

A woman can only be one flesh with one man at a time, but a man can be one flesh with more than one woman at a time. There is nothing a man can do to stop being one flesh with a woman he made love to. Making love to another woman won't end his union with any previous woman. But if a woman who is one flesh with a man, makes love to another man, her becoming one flesh with him, ends her one-flesh union with the previous man.

Based on the foregoing, although marriage is the only proper place for the one-flesh union, there are periods when the two things exist separately from each other. For example, Adam and Eve were one flesh before they were married, since Eve was made from a piece taken out of Adam.

Usually, men and women become one flesh after becoming married via a wedding ceremony. Also, unless the one-flesh union was already broken via adultery, divorced couples continue to be one flesh after divorce, until the x-wife commits fornication or marries someone else.

The following scenarios help us think about the one-flesh union separately from the marriage relationship.

Unmarried Woman One Flesh with No Man
Virgins, and widows who have not had physical relations with any man after their deceased husbands, are not one flesh with any man, and should stay that way unless and until they marry. 2 Cor. 11:2, "I have espoused you to one husband, that I may present you as a chaste virgin to Messiah."

Married, Including Remarried, Woman One
Flesh with Her Husband
Married, including remarried, women should remain one flesh with their husbands. Rom. 7:3, "If, while her husband lives, she is married to another man [becoming one flesh with him and thus ending her previous one-flesh union], she shall be called an adulteress."

Married, Including Remarried, Woman One Flesh with a Man Other than Her Husband

It's possible for a woman to be married to one man, but one flesh with another via adultery. Adultery breaks the one-flesh union by establishing a new one-flesh union, but it doesn't break the marriage; only divorce can do that. Whenever the obligations of marriage and the one-flesh union conflict, the obligations of marriage take precedence, since the one-flesh union is only appropriate within marriage. Married women who are one flesh with another man, should stop having physical relations with him, and reestablish the one-flesh union with their husbands. The "marriage ... bed is undefiled," Heb. 13:4.

Unmarried Woman One Flesh with a Married Man

Biblically, it's irrelevant whether a man is already married; but practically today, a married man who becomes one flesh with an unmarried woman through fornication will normally have to send her away, like Sarah insisted Abraham do to Hagar (Gen. 21:9-14), for everyone's legal safety and welfare. And his sin of not offering to add her in marriage per Exodus 22:16, will mostly be laid on today's Bible teachers, that interpret the Bible according to our modern culture.

Unmarried Woman One Flesh with an Unmarried Man

Every instance of physical lovemaking to an unmarried woman is fornication, even if the man and woman are one flesh through previous lovemaking, because physical intimacy is appropriate only within marriage. The man and woman in this situation should realize that if they don't marry, an even more serious violation of the woman's chastity will occur when she becomes one flesh by marrying another man later. "If a man entice a maid that is not betrothed, and lie with her, he shall surely endow her to be his wife," Ex. 22:16.

But entering marriage is too life-changing a decision to be decided on the basis of the one-flesh union alone. If an unmarried woman were to wake up one morning, and find she had made love to an abusive stranger because she got drunk the night before, she shouldn't marry him. Men and women should consider the harm has already done through fornication, rather than let one bad decision lead to another by marrying into a bad match. And no woman should marry or remarry a man who would fail to provide safety, food, clothing, and lovemaking, because failure to provide those things gives a wife the right to divorce anyway (Ex. 21:10-11).

Paul said, "The body is not for fornication, but for the Lord. ... Don't you know that he which is joined to a harlot is one body? For two, said he, shall be one flesh," 1 Cor. 6:13, 16. But Paul didn't then go on to say whoever commits fornication with a harlot should marry her.

Mt 5:28. Adultery by Lusting After a Woman

In Matthew chapters 5-7, known as the "sermon on the mount," Jesus didn't contradict the Law, but gave it the full and proper interpretation it should always have had. "Think not that I am come to destroy the law or the prophets," Mt. 5:17.

He corrected the Pharisee's focus on the external technicalities of the Law. "I say to you, that except your righteousness shall exceed the righteousness of the scribes and Pharisees, you will in no case enter into the kingdom of heaven," Mt. 5:20. The Law requires inward, not just external, righteousness. All sins are ultimately sins of the heart, because that's where they originate. "Out of the heart proceed evil thoughts, murders, adulteries, fornications, thefts, false witness, blasphemies," Mt. 5:19-20.

Every sin can be classified under one of the ten commandments, and the ten commandments can be classified under two commandments. "You shall love the Lord your God with all your heart [the first four commandments]; ... and ... you shall love your neighbor as yourself [the last six]. On these two commandments hang all the law and the prophets," Mt. 22:37-40.

Mt. 5:27-28. You have heard that it was said by them of old time, 'You shall not commit adultery;' but I say to you, that whoever looks on a woman to lust after her has committed adultery with her already in his heart.

Regarding the seventh commandment, Jesus wasn't saying that even looking at your own wife with lust is adultery, because the tenth commandment says, "You shall not lust after your neighbor's wife," Ex. 20:17. As for their own wives, husbands are obligated to look with desire on them. Someone has said "man desires woman, and woman desires the desire of a man." In God's lovemaking manual in the Bible, Solomon's wife rejoices that "I am my beloved's, and his desire is toward me," Song 7:10. So the "woman" referred to in Matthew 5:28 excludes one's own wife.

And the woman lusted after doesn't have to be married or engaged for it to be adultery rather than fornication. All sins relating to immorality, whether internal or external, lust of action or of thought, fornication or adultery, can be grouped under the seventh commandment. Jesus was teaching that the seventh commandment is broken by more than just the technical commission of the act of adultery according to the 'letter of the law.' All sins of immorality are the same kind of sin as adultery, though they're not all of the same degree or manifestation. So lusting after a woman other than your wife violates the seventh commandment. It's not sin to have the thought cross your mind, but it is sin to nurture it rather than turning from it to better thoughts.

Mt 5:31-32a; Deut 24:1-4. Adultery by Divorcing a Wife

Mt. 5:31. It has been said, "Whoever shall put away his wife, let him give her a writing of divorcement."

Matthew 5:31-32 are Jesus' commentary on Deuteronomy 24, the main passage in the Law about a husband divorcing a wife. It said if a husband divorced a wife, he had to give her a written document of divorce, so she would have legal proof she was free to remarry. The ability to remarry is important for a woman, not only to avoid fornication, but also for her protection, provision, and bearing children to care for her in her old age.

"When a man has taken a wife, and married her,

and it come to pass that she finds no favor in his eyes, because he has found some uncleanness in her; then let him write her a bill of divorcement, and give it in her hand, and send her out of his house. And when she is departed out of his house, she may go and be another man's wife. And if the latter husband hate her, and write her a bill of divorcement, and gives it in her hand, and sends her out of his house; or if the latter husband die, which took her to be his wife; her former husband, which sent her away, may not take her again to be his wife, after that she is defiled; for that is abomination before the Lord, and you shall not cause the land to sin, which the Lord your God gives you for an inheritance," Deut. 24:1-4.

The Hebrew phrase for "uncleanness" here is "ervat dabar," meaning a "nakedness thing." The rabbis debated over whether this phrase referred to a sexual sin, or to pretty much anything. "House of Shammai says, 'A man may not divorce his wife unless he finds out about her having engaged in a matter of forbidden sexual intercourse [devar erva], i.e., she committed adultery or is suspected of doing so.' ... And House of Hillel says, 'He may divorce her even due to a minor issue, e.g., because she burned or over-salted his dish, as it is stated, 'Because he has found some unseemly matter in her,' meaning that he found any type of shortcoming in her.'

Rabbi Akiva says, 'He may divorce her even if he found another woman who is better looking than her and wishes to marry her, as it is stated in that verse, 'And it comes to pass, if she finds no favor in his eyes,''" Talmud, Gittan 90a.

But burning toast is not 'a nakedness thing.' "Uncleanness" in Deuteronomy 24:1, refers to any kind of sexual immorality, or "fornication," as Yeshua said in Matthew 5:32a. A husband has the right to expect his wife won't have physical relations with any other man. There is no other biblical reason for a man to divorce his wife, and biblically there would be no need for a man to divorce for anything less, because he would always be free to add another wife, but in societies like ours that prohibit polygyny, additional practical reasons, like for abandonment, become valid.

Notice that although a divorced woman is permitted to remarry another, she is still "defiled," Deut. 24:4, by doing so. It's not possible for a woman to be married and one flesh with one man, and later become married and one flesh with another man, thus breaking her one-flesh union with her x-husband while he still lives, without her chastity being violated.

Notice also, a divorced woman is never permitted to remarry any former husband except her last one. Once she remarries another, she can't return to a previous husband even if "the latter husband die," Deut. 24:3. The world and many pastors might think it's a beautiful thing for a woman to return to a previous husband after marrying another, but God sees it as "abomination," Deut. 24:4. A sin like: "If a man lie with his daughter in law, ... they have wrought confusion. ... If a man also lie with mankind, ... both of them have committed an abomination. ... If a man take a wife and her mother, it is wickedness," Lev. 20:12-14.

On the other hand, notice there's no prohibition against marrying a new <u>subsequent</u> husband if her husband divorces her or dies. She is defiled in regards to her former husband by her marriage to another, but her latter marriage is as "honorable and undefiled," Heb. 13:4, as her former marriage was, so we see divorce frees her to remarry anyone except any husband previous to the one that last divorced her.

Finally, notice there wasn't any need for Moses to mention that the husband who divorced his wife could remarry. Men are already allowed to have more than one wife without violating chastity, and the husband might already have more than one wife. Only the marital status of the woman is relevant as to whether a man and woman can marry.

Mt. 5:32a. But I say to you that, whoever shall put away his wife, saving for the cause of fornication, causes her to commit adultery.

Jesus' point is that even when a husband provides the legal divorce papers required by Deuteronomy 24:2, it doesn't mean no one is harmed, and no sin is committed. As in the other parts of Matthew 5, Jesus corrected the misinterpretations of the Law that resulted from focusing on the external technicalities instead of on the underlying morality. The Jewish rabbis focused on providing a 'writ,' but Jesus said every time a husband divorces a wife, either the husband or the wife is guilty of adultery.

The exception clause, "saving for the cause of fornication," isn't there to provide a valid reason for divorce. It's there to determine who is guilty of adultery. A wife who didn't commit adultery is still one flesh with the husband who divorced her, so he will bear the guilt of endangering her chastity at divorce, and its future violation at her remarriage. A wife who did commit adultery, is already guilty of severing the one-flesh union with her husband, so in that case, she will bear her own guilt. The 'exception clause,' uses the word 'fornication,' instead of 'adultery,' to include lesser sexual sins besides the actual act of adultery.

Notice the husband in this verse causes his wife to commit adultery by <u>divorcing</u> her, "whoever shall put away his wife ... causes her to commit adultery," Mt. 5:32a, even if she never remarries. He is guilty of abandoning his duty to protect his wife's chastity. Attempted murder is just as bad as murder from the perspective of the person who commits it, though it's not as bad for the intended victim. And reckless endangering is still a crime, even if the endangered person escapes injury.

When a husband divorces his wife he makes it so she must violate her chastity to be married. He puts her in a position where the only way she can perform her special ministry of chastity to give herself to only one man as long as he lives, would be to stay single until her x-husband dies. But she's also required to remarry to avoid fornication, and to receive the provisions and affection she's entitled to.

When a man marries, he becomes responsible to provide a safe place for his wife to maintain her chastity and purity. "Husbands, love your wives, even as Messiah also loved the church, and gave himself for it, so that he could sanctify and cleanse it with the washing of water by the word, so that he could present it to himself a glorious church, not having spot, or wrinkle, or any such thing, but that it should be holy and without blemish," Eph.

5:25-27.

A husband isn't permitted to share his wife. "Drink waters out of your own cistern, and running waters out of your own well. ... Let them be only your own, and not be for strangers with you. Let your fountain be blessed: and rejoice with the wife of your youth. Let her be as the loving hind and pleasant roe. Let her breasts satisfy you at all times, and be ravished always with her love," Prov. 5:15-19.

A husband is required to help his wife stay pure by providing lovemaking for her. "To avoid fornication, ... let the husband render to the wife due benevolence. ... The husband has not power of his own body, but the wife. Don't defraud one the other, ... so that Satan doesn't tempt you for your incontinency," 1 Cor. 7:2-5.

Matthew 5:32 says a husband who divorces his wife "causes her to commit adultery." It's the person who causes something who bears the guilt. A person can't be held responsible for something someone else caused. God lays the guilt of the adultery that will occur when she remarries, on the husband at the time he causes it by divorcing his wife, whether or not she ever remarries.

When she does remarry, her marriage is as holy and pure as every other marriage, even though her previous one-flesh union will be severed at the consummation of her remarriage. Like for David and Bathsheba, "marriage is honorable in all, and the bed undefiled," Heb. 13:4. There are no "remarriages" in the Bible, only marriages.

Mt 5:32b. Adultery by Marrying a Divorced Woman

Mt. 5:32b. And whoever shall marry her that is divorced commits adultery.

The Bible consistently says that whoever marries a divorced woman, assuming she had not made love to another man after her husband, commits adultery, and there's never an 'exception clause,' for it. The new husband violates the divorced woman's chastity when he severs her previous one-flesh union by becoming one flesh with her, either at the consummation of her remarriage, or when he committed adultery with her before her remarriage.

If a divorced woman is still one flesh with her x-husband, and if there's still much chance for reconciliation, and if her x-husband would be a good husband, then a man should be very careful about coming between a divorced woman and her x-husband. If he marries her, he prevents her from ever returning to her previous husband per

Deuteronomy 24:4. On the other hand, biblically, even her x-husband's remarriage doesn't prevent her from returning to him as an additional wife, though, practically, it usually does in our society today.

A man doesn't incur guilt by marrying a divorced woman even though he commits adultery with her by doing so. He does a kind and good thing to marry her, and it's God's will that "to avoid fornication, ... let every woman [including divorced women] have her own husband," 1 Cor. 7:2. Either the woman's x-husband or the divorced woman herself (per Matthew 5:32a), will bear the guilt, as long as the new husband wasn't complicit in the pre-divorce fornication that led to her divorce.

The 'Invalid Divorce' Misinterpretation

Mt. 5:32. Whoever shall put away his wife, except for the cause of fornication, causes her to commit adultery; and whoever shall marry her that is divorced commits adultery.

The 'invalid divorce' misinterpretation of Jesus' divorce and remarriage teaching has caused immense harm over the centuries. One version of the 'invalid divorce' misinterpretation says a divorce for any reason less than fornication is invalid, and thus the couple is still married, and any remarriages are invalid, and so physical relations with the new person who is not really a new spouse is actually continual adultery.

But marriage can't survive divorce. Only the one-flesh union can survive divorce. The adultery Jesus said occurs at remarriage doesn't occur because the divorced couple remains married after the divorce, but because they remain one flesh after the divorce.

"If, while [the man who was] her husband lives, she is married to another man, she shall be called an adulteress; but if [the man who was] her husband is dead, she is free from that law; so that she is no adulteress, though she is married to another man," Rm. 7:3. Whether there's a divorce or not, a wife remains one flesh with her husband until he dies; or until, while he still lives, she becomes one flesh with another man, which is adultery. The death of the husband, or the wife's glorification at the return of the Lord, are the only ways to end the one-flesh union that aren't adultery.

If the 'invalid divorce' misinterpretation was true, Matthew 5:32 would read, "Whoever thinks he puts away his wife, except for the cause of fornication, causes her to commit adultery; and whoever thinks he marries her he thinks is divorced commits adultery," Mt. 5:32.

Jesus recognized divorces and remarriages even when the divorce wasn't for fornication. "I say to you, 'Whoever shall PUT AWAY his wife, except it be for fornication, and shall MARRY another, commits adultery; and whoever MARRIES her which is PUT AWAY, commits adultery,'" Mt. 19:9. He said they really "put away" and they really "marry," even when the divorce isn't based on fornication.

Jesus didn't tell the Samaritan woman at the well, "you have had one real husband, and the last four whom you've had were not really husbands, and he whom you now have is also not your husband." He said "you have had five husbands, and he whom you now have is not your husband," Jn. 4:18, because she was living with the man without marrying him. And Jesus didn't tell her to go back to her 'first and only true' husband. He told her to stop sinning, which she could do by marrying the man she was living with or stop living with him.

The purpose of the writ of divorce in Deuteronomy 24 was to protect the right of divorced wives to remarry. As long as a woman had a writ, no one could question if she was free to remarry. "Let him write her a bill of divorcement, and give it in her hand, ... and when she is departed out of his house, she may go and be another man's wife," Deut. 24:1-2. If divorces for invalid reasons were not valid divorces, no one would know if a writ was valid, and writs would be worthless, and women would lose the protection they provided to remarry.

The Talmud has a whole tractate in the Book of Women about what constitutes a valid writ of divorce, but the rabbis rightly focus on the writ itself, not on what the reasons for the divorce might have been. Unfortunately, they also made the rules about the form and delivery of the writ too complicated. Biblically, the husband only had to write a writ of divorce, and put it in his wife's hand. Perhaps God wanted the husband to "give it in her hand," Deut. 24:1, because seeing her face while he gives it to her might make him have compassion and change his mind.

Perhaps God intentionally left the reasons for divorce in Deuteronomy 24 open to a wide range of interpretation, to avoid all discussion of whether a divorce was made for valid reasons, to better protect the right of women to remarry. Some possible reasons for divorce in the passage are, "it come to pass that she find no favor in his eyes," "he hath found some uncleanness in her," or he "hate her," Deut. 24:1-3.

Yeshua was referring to "some uncleanness"

[ervat dabar, nakedness thing], Deut. 24:1, meaning sexual uncleanness, when he said "except it be for fornication," Mt. 5:32; 19:9. But Yeshua didn't say the writ isn't valid if the divorce isn't for fornication; he said the divorcing husband is the one guilty of adultery if the divorce isn't for fornication. Once again, the 'exception clause' isn't there to enumerate the valid reasons for divorce, but to determine who bears the guilt of the adultery caused by the divorce.

Those who believe a divorce for an invalid reason isn't a valid divorce can't even agree among themselves what the valid reason is. Is it any kind of sexual sin, or adultery only, or fornication during engagement only, or incest only, etc.? Don't you think something so important would be stated more clearly if it could make the whole thing invalid?

A divorced woman has no more marriage connection to an x-husband than a widow does. "If a woman ... vow a vow to the Lord, ... but if her husband disallowed her, ... then he shall make her vow which she vowed ... of none effect. ... But every vow of <u>a widow and of her that is divorced</u> which with they have bound their souls shall stand against her," Num. 30:3-9. What a mess if the reasons for every woman's divorce would have to be evaluated to figure out if she has the authority to bind herself before making a business contract with her, for example.

Men that teach divorces are invalid if they're made for invalid reasons, teach exactly the opposite of what the Bible says. The Bible says "Let him write her a bill of divorcement, ... and when she is departed out of his house, she may go and be another man's wife," Deut. 24:1-2, but they say she can't go and be another man's wife. The Bible says "if the latter husband ... write her a bill of divorcement, ... her former husband ... may not take her again to be his wife," but they say remarried couples should leave their current spouses and return to their previous, 'real' spouses. The Bible says God "hates putting away," Mal. 2:16, but they say God wants remarried people to divorce each other.

The Bible says "to avoid fornication, let every man have his own wife, and let every woman have her own husband," but they say, most divorced people can never have a husband or wife again. The Bible says, "I say therefore to the unmarried, ... if they cannot contain, let them marry," but they say, don't let them marry. The Bible says "marriage is honorable and the bed undefiled," Heb. 13:4, but they say, marriage is not honorable and undefiled for people who remarry. The 'invalid divorce' teachers cause the same kind of harm as those that "depart from the faith, ... forbidding to marry," 1 Tim. 4:3, because they forbid the use of God's provision for avoiding fornication.

God didn't have the prophet Nathan command David to divorce Bathsheba, even though he committed adultery with her, and had her husband murdered. Once they were married, regardless of the sordid, sinful path that led to that marriage, from that time forward, they were in an "honorable ... and undefiled," Heb. 13:4, marriage; and Solomon and the kings of Judah and Yeshua were the descendants of that marriage.

The 'invalid divorce' teaching makes it better for people to have sinned, than not to have sinned. If your spouse did commit adultery and divorced you, the divorce counts, and you can get remarried; but if your spouse didn't commit adultery and divorced you, the divorce doesn't count, and you can't get remarried. So, it's better for you if your spouse committed adultery, which the Bible would never say.

Most 'invalid divorce' teachers deny remarriage to the guilty party even when they claim the divorce counts. Jesus didn't say anything about this in the divorce and remarriage passages. The need to go beyond what the Bible says to try to make things fair is a clue the whole interpretation is wrong. Hopefully, few people actually follow this teaching, but unfortunately it does the most harm to the most conscientious. Common sense is better than false teaching.

A few Bible teachers deny remarriage to the guilty party, because the guilty party has the 'unfinished moral business of repentance' to do. This isn't in the divorce teachings of Jesus, unless it's hidden in middle voiced participles or something, which the average person has no chance of understanding. They use passages like Jer. 3:1; Is. 50:1; Hos. 1-2, Mt. 1:19; 18:15ff to add this 'missing feature' to Jesus' teaching.

They call the divorce a 'disciplinary divorce;' a kind of 'tough love,' to bring the parties back together. But divorce is moving in the wrong direction. Even separation makes it less likely a couple will ever reconcile, especially combined with the common practice for women to proclaim 'no contact' in such situations; and divorce makes reconciliation far, far less likely.

For some reason, I can't find dependable data about what percentage of separated and divorced couples reconcile. Some web pages quote <u>The Lost Love Chronicles</u> by Dr. Nancy Kalish in 2006, but her study was about lost childhood romances, and the number of participants was small. I couldn't find statistics in her book of stories about reunited, long-lost lovers; but she is reported to have said 13% of separated couples reconcile, and 6% [of the 50% of divorced couples who remarry, i.e. 3%], remarry their x-spouses. Her website says, "This is still the only research book that has ever been published on actual reunited couples," and that's believable.

Some websites mention Michele Weiner-Davis who said in 2010 that as many as 10% of divorced couples remarry their x-spouses. However, she owns a "Divorce Busting" business, so she has reasons to present as high a reconciliation rate as possible.

One family law website, Wilkinson & Finkbeiner, said, "in 2011, only 29 out of every 1000 [3%] of divorced or widowed women remarried" at all, never mind to their x-spouses. And they reportedly "wait an average of three years after a divorce to remarry (if they remarry at all)," so maybe that means about 9% eventually remarry?

A Pew Research Center report dated 11/14/2014 said 20% of new marriages involve remarriages for both spouses. If only 13% of those remarriages are couples that remarry their X, that's 2.6% of divorced couples who reconcile and remarry. If only 50% of divorced couples remarry at all, that's about 1.3% of divorced couples who reconcile.

Whatever the exact statistics, separation and divorce lead in the opposite direction to reconciliation. God may divorced the northern kingdom of Israel; but only God can divorce knowing all will be restored in the end. And 'disciplinary divorce' is sometimes taught as being mandatory! If God treated us like that, would any of us endure unto eternal life?

Lu 16:18; Ex 21:10. Adultery by Neglecting a Wife

Lu. 16:17-18. It is easier for heaven and earth to pass, than one tittle of the law to fail. Whoever puts away his wife, and marries another, commits adultery; and whoever marries her that is put away from her husband commits adultery.

In Luke 17, Jesus condemned the Pharisees for their poor stewardship of the Law, and he gave one representative example; their misuse of the Law regarding divorce. The Pharisees thought all was well, so long as they followed the steps Moses prescribed in Deuteronomy 24, but Jesus said it's adultery for a man to divorce his wife and remarry.

Since the biblical definition of adultery permits a man to have more than one wife at one time, how could it be relevant whether a man marries another after divorcing his wife? Some teachers believe that by saying these three words, "and marries another," Jesus made remarriage a relevant consideration for men, and thereby changed the Old Testament definition of adultery, invalidated writs of divorce, and outlawed polygamy. But Yeshua wouldn't have made such drastic changes in such an indirect and unclear way. If Jesus had wanted to change the definition of adultery, invalidate writs of divorce, and prohibit polygamy, this would have been a very cryptic way to do so. Such major changes in people's lives would have merited a few explicit commands.

The ASV says Jesus rescinded the Mosaic dietary laws simply by saying "there is nothing from without the man, that going into him can defile him. ... This he said, making all meats clean," ASV, Mk. 7:15, 19. But the disciples didn't start eating pork after that statement. God made it clear we're not under the law by giving us Acts 15, Romans 6-8a, Galatians, Ephesians, Colossians, Hebrews, etc.; not merely a hint in passing.

The phrase "and shall marry another," doesn't refer to Deuteronomy 24:1-4, because that passage doesn't talk about men marrying. Rather it refers to Exodus 21:2-11, because that's the passage about men remarrying. It's the main passage in the Law about women's marriage and divorce rights, with voluminous commentary about it in rabbinic writings.

"If a man sell his daughter to be a maidservant, she shall not go out [after six years of service] as the menservants do. If she please not her master, who has betrothed her to himself, then he shall let her be redeemed. ... If he take him another wife; her food, her raiment, and her duty of marriage, shall he not diminish. And if he do not these three to her, then she shall go out free without money," Ex. 21:2-11.

Although these verses are about the rights of a maidservant who married her master, the rabbis rightly reasoned that if maidservants had these rights, then free women had them even more. "Included in this negative commandment are all daughters of Israel (as well), not to reduce from them anything from these [food, clothing, and lovemaking]. [This inclusion] is a fortiori. ... If [a man may] not reduce for [bondwomen], all the more so for free [women]. ... It is written [in Ex. 21:9], "like the statute of the daughters [freewomen] he shall do for her." [This passage] came to learn [from the statutes of the daughters], but it ends up to teach, as the [law of the] daughters are learned from her [the bondwoman]," Sefer HaChinukh 46.

Exodus 21:2-11 is about a man marrying another wife, and then failing to provide for his earlier wife; whereas Luke 16:18 is about a man failing to provide for his earlier wife by divorcing her, and then marrying another. But God can see through the legal fictions we create. It's even worse for a husband to divorce and thereby provide no care for his earlier wife, than to marry another and then provide inadequate care for his earlier wife.

Exodus 21:10-11 says a woman is entitled to food, clothing (including things like shelter and safety), and physical love, including the possibility of children to care for her in her old age. If a husband doesn't provide those things, a wife had the right to petition the courts to force her husband to divorce her, so she could marry someone else who would. "If he is not willing to divorce the woman, ... flog him ... until he divorces her," Rashi on Lev. 21:8. Inconveniently, for those who oppose polygamy, this passage regulating polygamy, "if he take him another wife," Ex. 21:10, is the only passage in the Bible about the marriage and divorce rights of women for their protection.

The rabbis interpreted "food, clothing, and shelter," to be more than those things specifically. "How [is he obligated] for her clothing? He must give her clothes fit for the rainy months, and for the sunny months. ... Among the clothes that he must give her is included her household vessels: ... a bed with a spread, and a mat ... to sit on, and utensils for food such as a dish and a pot and a jug and a flask, a lamb, a cup, a bottle and other such things. The residence that he rents for her, must be a house measuring [at least] six by six feet, with a courtyard outside of it, and a toilet room is not considered part of this measure. And we make him give her adornments like colorful clothing to put around her head and forehead, and eyeshadow, ... and rouge ... [for her] face, ... and other such things. To what does this refer? To a poor Jew. But a rich person must provide her with all of these things in accord with his wealth. If he was cheap in providing for her, even a poor Jew, we force him to divorce her. And the marriage contract amount will be a debt over his head until he grows wealthier," Shulchan Aruch, Even HaEzer 73:1-5.

Per Deuteronomy 24, a husband is entitled to his wife's faithfulness, and he can divorce her for "[sexual] uncleanness," Deut. 24:1, but not for any failure to receive food, clothing, and lovemaking from her. On the other hand, per Exodus 21, a wife is entitled to food, clothing, and lovemaking from her husband, and she can force him to divorce her if he doesn't provide these for her, but not for "[sexual] uncleanness," Deut. 24:1, or for "fornication," Mt. 5:32; 19:9. A wife is not entitled to a husband's exclusivity in the Law, because husbands are permitted to have more than one wife.

However, in modern times, a wife may, by her influence or by contract, require her husband's exclusivity. After Rabbi Gershom outlawed polygamy within Sephardic Judaism about 1000 AD, the rabbis said, "in a place where they are accustomed to only marry one woman, he is not permitted to marry another woman in addition to his wife without her permission, and certainly if he stipulated in her Ketuba (marriage contract) that he would not marry another woman in addition to her," Shulchan Aruch, Even HaEzer 76:8.

The Pharisees thought if a man failed to provide for his wife per Exodus 21:10, but gave her a writ of divorce per Exodus 21:11, that made everything ok. "A man who rebels against his wife and says, 'I will feed and support her, but will not have sexual relations with her because I hate her,' we add the value of 36 barleycorns of silver to her ketuba (marriage contract) each week, and he remains without relations as long as she is willing to wait. Even though her ketuba amount continues to grow, he is still transgressing a negative commandment, as it says, 'he shall not withhold' (Ex. 21:10). If she so desires, [the] court can force him to divorce her immediately, and to give her the ketuba money. ... If he wants to divorce her immediately and give her ketuba, ... it seems to me that in such a case he also does not transgress the negative commandment of 'he shall not withhold,'" Shulchan Aruch, Even HaEzer 77:1.

But even though a wife has the right to a divorce under Ex. 21:11, her chastity will still be violated when she severs her one-flesh union with her x-husband by becoming one flesh with another man at her remarriage. And apart from the exception clause of Mt. 5:32 and 19:9, God will put the guilt of the adultery from her remarriage on her x-husband's account, because he's the one who put her in the position of having to leave him to have her needs provided for.

The ten commandments all have both negative and positive aspects. The seventh commandment 'prohibits' immorality, but it also 'requires' positive aspects of purity. "To avoid fornication, ... let the husband render to the wife due benevolence," 1 Cor. 7:2-3. Even if a husband doesn't divorce his wife, he commits adultery against her chastity if he doesn't provide her "duty of marriage," Ex. 21:10, because he forces her to have to divorce him to have her appropriate needs met.

The rabbis taught sex is a woman's right, and a man's obligation. "[Regarding] a man who forbade himself by vow from having intercourse with his wife, Beth Shammai says [he can abstain for] two weeks [sounds like 1 Cor. 7:5]; Beth Hillel says one week. ... The times for conjugal duty prescribed in the Torah are: for independent men, every day; for workers, twice a week; for donkey-drivers, once a week; for camel-drivers, once in thirty days; for sailors, once in six months [because their work keeps them away longer]," Talmud, Ketubot 61b.

Luke 16:18 and the other divorce and remarriage verses emphasize the actions of men, even though men are always free to marry regardless of their marital status. The two men mentioned in Luke 16:18, the divorcing x-husband and the remarrying new husband, both commit adultery, not because they violate their own chastity, but because of how they affect the chastity of the woman.

Mt 19:1-8; Mk 10:1-9. It's Never Right to Divorce a Wife

Mt. 19:1-3. Jesus ... came into the borders of Judaea beyond Jordan. ... The Pharisees also came to him, tempting him, and saying to him, "Is it lawful for a man to put away his wife for every cause?"

Mk. 10:1-2. He ... came into the borders of Judaea by the farther side of Jordan. ... And the Pharisees came to him, and asked him, "Is it lawful for a man to put away his wife?" tempting him.

Matthew 19 and Mark 10 record parallel accounts of the same event. A little earlier, in Luke 16:18, Jesus had told the Pharisees that every husband who divorces his wife and marries another commits adultery. So now the Pharisees came asking, "Is it lawful for a man to put away his wife?" Mt. 19:3; Mk. 10:2, hoping Jesus would publicly contradict Moses by saying divorce is unlawful so they could condemn his ministry.

Mk. 10:3-4. And he answered and said to them, "What did Moses command you?" And they said, "Moses permitted to write a bill of divorcement, and to put her away."

In Mark's account, Jesus asked what Moses commanded, and the Pharisees rightly replied that Moses didn't 'command' divorce, he only 'permitted' it in Deuteronomy 24. God permits men to divorce their wives to protect women from even worse cruel things men might do to them to be free of them. He didn't give Deuteronomy 24:1-4 to provide a list of valid reasons for divorce, but to require writs of divorce, to protect divorced women, by enabling them to prove they were free and available for remarriage. He probably also permits divorce to avoid problems like they have in the Catholic-dominated Philippines, where because divorce is wrongly illegal, many married couples separate and live with other partners outside of wedlock, and the latter relationships are even less permanent than the former, because they can't marry.

Mk. 10:5-9. And Jesus answered and said to them, "For the hardness of your heart he wrote you this precept. But from the beginning of the creation God made them male and female. For this cause shall a man leave his father and mother, and cleave to his wife, and they two shall be one flesh. So then they are no more two, but one flesh. What therefore God has joined together, let not man put asunder."

Mt. 19:4-6. He answered and said to them, "Have you not read, that he which made them at the beginning made them male and female, and said, 'For this cause shall a man leave father and mother, and shall cleave to his wife, and they two shall be one flesh?' Therefore they are no longer two, but one flesh. What therefore God has joined together, let not man put asunder."

Jesus' answered it's never right for a husband to divorce his wife. Even if you give your wife a writ of divorce so she can remarry, you're still guilty of "hardness of heart" (Mk. 10:5). The important thing to notice is he gave his complete answer at this point and stopped talking. He didn't need to mention any 'exception clause' for fornication. If the Pharisees or the disciples hadn't gone on to ask more questions, that would have been the end of the conversation.

Also notice Jesus didn't talk about breaking marriage contracts, marriage covenants, or marriage vows in his answer. Marriage is to protect the one-flesh union. Divorce puts the one-flesh union at risk of being "put asunder," Mk. 10:9; Mt. 19:6, and sundering the one-flesh union of a married woman is adultery.

Mt. 19:7-8. They said to him, "Why did Moses then command to give a writing of divorcement, and to put her away?" He said to them, "Moses, because of the hardness of your hearts, permitted you to put away your wives; but from the beginning it wasn't so."

In Matthew's account, it's the Pharisees who asked why Moses 'commanded' divorce, and Jesus who pointed out Moses only 'permitted' it. God permits divorce for the protection of women because of the hardness of men's hearts. Even when a husband isn't guilty of causing his wife to commit adultery by divorcing her, because she already committed adultery; he's still guilty of "hardness of heart," Mt. 19:8; Mk. 10:5.

And hardness of heart falls under the sixth commandment (Mt. 5:21-22), "You shall not kill," Ex. 20:13. To divorce a wife is to "hate her," Deut. 24:3. Every man who divorces his wife is minimally guilty of hardness of heart, hatred, lack of love, unkindness, unforgiveness, cruelty, treachery, violence, and of doing what God hates (Mal. 2:14-16); even when he's not also guilty of endangering her chastity. "Peter ... said, 'Lord, how often shall my brother sin against me, and I forgive him? Until seven times?' Jesus said to him, 'I don't say to you until seven times; but until seventy times seven,'" Mt. 18:21-22.

"The LORD has been a witness between you and the wife of your youth, against whom you have dealt treacherously. Yet she is your companion, and the wife of your covenant. And did not he make one [flesh, Gen. 2:24]? ... Therefore take heed to your spirit, and let none deal treacherously against the wife of his youth. For the LORD, the God of Israel, says that he hates divorce, for one covers violence with his garment," Mal. 4:13-16.

Mk. 10:10-12. And in the house his disciples asked him again of the same matter. And he said to them, "Whoever shall put away his wife, and marry another, commits adultery against her. And if a woman shall put away her husband,

and be married to another, she commits adultery."

Mt. 19:9. And I say to you, "Whoever shall put away his wife, except it be for fornication, and shall marry another, commits adultery; and whoever marries her which is put away commits adultery."

According to Mark, these verses were spoken to the disciples "in the house," without the Pharisees present. Jesus had already given his complete statement to the Pharisees, that although Moses did provide laws to minimize the damage to women from divorce, it's never right for a man to divorce his wife.

We already dealt with the exception clause of Matthew 19:9a, "except it be for fornication," in the section on Matthew 5:31-32a about "Adultery by Divorcing a Wife."

And we already dealt with Mark 10:11, "Whoever shall put away his wife, <u>and marry another,</u> commits adultery;" and Matthew 19:9a, "Whoever shall put away his wife, ... <u>and shall marry another,</u> commits adultery;" in the section on Luke 16:18 about 'Adultery by Neglecting a Wife."

And we will deal with Mark 10:12, "And if a woman shall put away her husband, and be married to another, she commits adultery," in the following section about "Adultery by Divorcing a Husband and Remarrying."

The only additional information to deal with here is the extra clause "against her" in Mark 10:11, "Whoever shall put away his wife, and marry another, commits adultery against her." There is nothing a husband can do himself to end his one-flesh union with his wife. He can't sunder it by marrying another wife. Men can only be chaste based on how they treat the chastity of women. By divorcing and remarrying, an x-husband commits adultery <u>against</u> his x-wife, by failing to continue to provide her food, clothing, and lovemaking when taking another wife per Exodus 21:10, which puts her in the position of needing to remarry to receive those things.

But for the wife who divorces her husband, Mark simply says "she commits adultery," Mk. 10:12; not, "she commits adultery against him," because she herself severs their one-flesh union by becoming one flesh with another man by remarrying.

Mt. 19:10-12. His disciples said to him, "If the case of the man is so with his wife, it is not good to marry." But he said to them, "All men can't receive this saying, except them to whom it is given. For there are some eunuchs, which were so born from their mother's womb, and there are some eunuchs which were made eunuchs of men, and there are eunuchs which have made themselves eunuchs for the kingdom of heaven's sake. He that is able to receive it, let him receive it."

The interpretation of Matthew 19:3-9 and Mark 10:1-9, that says Jesus taught it's never right for a man to divorce his wife, is confirmed by the reaction of the disciples, who said, if that's the case, it's better for a man not to marry. Jesus agreed the standard is high, and that marriage requires the grace of God, but he said celibacy also requires the grace of God.

This interpretation is also confirmed in 1 Corinthians 7, where Paul says, "Unto the married, ... the Lord [commanded], ... let not the husband put away his wife," 1 Cor. 7:10-11. There's no exception clause; it's immoral for a man to divorce his wife.

In Ezra 10, Ezra made the people divorce their foreign wives, even those with children, but he was wrong to do so. Nowhere does the Bible say he was right to do so, and shortly after that event, the prophet Malachi remonstrated, "the God of Israel says that he hates putting away," Mal. 2:16. I think God recorded this event, without immediate comment, as an exercise for us to realize they erred.

Like when Jephthah killed his daughter so he wouldn't be guilty of breaking a foolish vow (Jdg. 11:30-40). Or when Israel nearly wiped out the tribe of Benjamin (Jdg. 19-21). Or when the drunken King Ahasuerus divorced Queen Vashti (Est. 1). Or when the apostles went beyond their apostolic authority and chose Matthias as a replacement for Judas instead of waiting for Jesus to select Paul as he did later (Acts 1:26; Gal. 1:1).

God's way is to never give up on his own. Even if God divorced the northern kingdom of Israel, he alone can divorce with the full assurance all will someday be restored. And he didn't divorce the southern kingdom of Judah even though she became one flesh with other gods. "They say, if a man divorce his wife, and she go from him, and become another man's, shall he return unto her again? Shall not that land be greatly polluted? But you have played the harlot with many lovers; yet return again to me, says the Lord, ... for I am married to you," Jer. 3:1-14.

God told Hosea to marry an unfaithful woman who would have children from other men; and told him to love her unconditionally, and win her heart in the end as a picture of God's unconditional, eternal acceptance of Israel and their eventual happy-ever-after marriage in the Messianic Kingdom.

"The Lord said to Hosea, 'Go, take unto you a wife of whoredoms and children of whoredoms; for the land has committed great whoredom, departing from the Lord.' So he went and took Gomer the daughter of Diblaim. ... She conceived, and bare a son. Then said God, 'Call his name Loammi [meaning 'not my people,' because he wasn't Hosea's child]; for you are not my people, and I will not be your God.' ... Yet ... it shall come to pass, that in the place where it was said unto them, 'You are not my people,' there it shall be said unto them, 'You are the sons of the living God.' ... [Hosea said,] 'Plead with your mother, plead: for she is not my wife, neither am I her husband; let her therefore put away her whoredoms.' ... Their mother has played the harlot. ... I will allure her, and bring her into the wilderness, and speak comfortably unto her, ... and she shall sing there, as in the days of her youth, and as in the day when she came up out of the land of Egypt. ... I will betroth you unto me forever," Hos. 1:1-2:23.

Some people interpret "she is not my wife, neither am I her husband," to mean Hosea divorced Gomer and remarried her later. I think Hosea was saying it was 'like' they weren't married. Israel didn't stop being God's people when he said "you are not my people, and I will not be your God." There has always been a believing remnant in every generation which is why Israel is preserved. "As the new wine is found in the cluster, and one says, 'Destroy it not; for a blessing is in it;' so will I do for my servants' sakes [the minority], that I may not destroy them all," Is. 65:8.

No matter how much Israel sins, God will never forsake her, because his love and commitment to her is unconditional. If we want to be like him, we must never forsake our wives, no matter what they do. "Thus says the Lord, which gives the sun for a light by day, and the ordinances of the moon and of the stars for a light by night, which divides the sea when the waves thereof roar. ... If those ordinances depart from before me, says the Lord, then the seed of Israel also shall cease from being a nation before me forever. ... If heaven above can be measured, and the foundations of the earth searched out beneath, I will also cast off all the seed of Israel for all that they have done, says the Lord," Jer. 31:35-37.

Also, "Thus says the Lord, if my covenant is not with day and night, and if I have not appointed the ordinances of heaven and earth, then will I cast away the seed of Jacob and David my servant, ... for I will cause their captivity to return, and have mercy on them," Jer. 33:25-26. If we have the mind of the Holy Spirit within us, then we must love our wives like God loves Israel, with an unconditional, unending love. God didn't divorce Israel before becoming engaged to the church, the bride of Messiah. He didn't violate Ex. 21:10, "If he take him another wife, her food, her raiment, and her duty of marriage, shall he not diminish."

Likewise, Messiah will never divorce his espoused bride, no matter what the church does. "I am persuaded, that neither death, nor life, nor angels, nor principalities, nor powers, nor things present, nor things to come, nor height, nor depth, nor any other creature, shall be able to separate us from the love of God, which is in Messiah Jesus our Lord," Rm. 8:38-39.

Marriage is so sacred to God that even when belief in Yeshua separates other family members, husband and wife should never be divided. "For I am come to set a man at variance against his father, and the daughter against her mother, and the daughter in law against her mother in law, [but he doesn't mention husband and wife]" Mt. 10:35. And even though God took everything from Job; his property, his children, and his health; he didn't take his wife from him.

Yeshua said it's always immoral and hardness of heart for a husband to divorce a wife. But that was during a time when society permitted polygamy, and a man could add a second wife without divorcing his first. Today, there are probably circumstances where a husband may need to divorce his wife, like for abandonment. And God will put the guilt of such divorces on the accounts of the Bible teachers who interpret the Bible according to modern culture, claim that polygyny is sin, and thus harm women's chastity and welfare, and separate families.

Mk 10:12. Adultery by Divorcing a Husband & Remarrying

Mk. 10: 12. And if a woman shall put away her husband, and be married to another, she commits adultery.

A wife commits adultery when she sunders the one-flesh union with her x-husband by becoming one flesh with another man at her remarriage. If she divorced her x-husband because he failed to provide, "her food, clothing, and duty of marriage (Ex. 21:10-11), then the guilt of her adultery will fall on her x-husband. If not, then she'll bear the guilt.

Notice there's never an exception clause, "except it be for fornication," for when a wife divorces her husband. You can't flip gender-specific verses around. The Bible says, "Whoever shall put away his wife, except it be for fornication, and shall marry another, commits adultery," Mt. 19:9; but never, "Whoever shall put away her husband, except it be for fornication, and shall marry another, commits adultery." A husband's fornication doesn't allow a wife to escape the guilt of her own adultery when she remarries.

Bible teachers today encourage precious, chaste wives to violate their own chastity, possibly for the first time in their lives, by telling them, that if a husband commits fornication, they can divorce him and marry another without being guilty of adultery. However, the guilt for the resulting destruction of families and the violation of the chastity of the divorcing wives, will be put on the account of the egalitarian Bible teachers, that flip gender-specific verses like Matthew 19:9 around.

A wife can't cause her husband to commit adultery by divorcing him, like a husband can his wife. "Whoever shall put away his wife ... causes her to commit adultery," Mt. 5:32; but never, "whoever shall put away her husband causes him to commit adultery," Mt. 5:32. Men can't commit adultery in remarriage, unless they marry a divorced woman. The gospels say three times that whoever marries a divorced woman commits adultery (Mt. 5:32, Mt. 19:9, Lu. 16:18), but never say whoever marries a divorced man commits adultery.

A woman who divorces her husband endangers

her own chastity. Biblically, she's free to return to her x-husband at any time, even if he remarries someone else, since the Bible permits polygyny, but not after she remarries someone else per Deut. 24:4. Practically though, because of today's teachers, an x-husband's remarriage prevents reconciliation.

Also, assuming the divorced woman had not made broken the one flesh union with her x-husband by making love to someone else before her new marriage partner, it's always true that "whoever shall marry her that is divorced commits adultery," Mt. 5:32. But if she divorced her x-husband because he failed to provide for her needs, the guilt of the new husband's adultery will fall on the x-husband; otherwise, the new husband's guilt will fall on her. But the new husband does a good thing by marrying her, and is not responsible for her being in the position of needing to remarry, so long as he wasn't complicit in how she got into that position.

Also, the Bible doesn't say a wife who divorces her husband is guilty of hardness of heart, like husbands are. "Moses because of the hardness of your hearts permitted you to put away your wives," Mt. 19:8; and never "Moses because of the hardness of your hearts permitted you to put away your husbands." Husbands have more power to influence the character of their marriages. A good husband can graciously help a wife of poor character improve, but even the best wife can't change an uncommitted or abusive husband.

God puts the responsibility of holding the marriage together on the husband. "Therefore shall a man leave his father and his mother, and shall cleave [hold] unto his wife: and they shall be one flesh," Gen. 2:24. It's the man that does the cleaving, and holds the couple together. If he lets go, the wife can't do his job for him to keep the marriage together, and her efforts will only be resented. But when a husband commits to holding the marriage together by loving his wife passionately, unselfishly, and unconditionally; when he's willing to climb mountains and swim oceans for her; few women would want to leave that kind of marriage.

The best a woman can do for her marriage is to make it as pleasant as possible for her husband by quiet submission. "Wives, be in subjection to your own husbands, that, if any obey not the word, they also may without the word [not by teaching, nagging, or trying to change him] be won by the behavior of the wives; while they behold your chaste behavior coupled with fear. Whose adorning let it ... be ... the ornament of a meek and quiet spirit, which is in the sight of God of great price. For after this manner in the old time the holy women also, who trusted in God, adorned themselves, being in subjection unto their own husbands. Even as Sara obeyed Abraham, calling him lord," 1 Pet. 1:1-3. But even for a perfect wife, if her husband lacks a conscientious character and commitment, he is likely to leave.

Jesus' Teaching Grouped by Phrase

JESUS' TEACHING ABOUT DIVORCE AND REMARRIAGE. One person per row bears the GUILT of the adultery.

	Woman Marries Divorced Husband	Husband Remarries Ex. 21:10	Husband Divorces Wife	Husband Commits Fornication	Wife Commits Fornication	Wife Divorces Husband	Wife Remarries Deut. 24:1-4	Man Marries Divorced Wife
Mt 5:32	never adultery	usually irrelevant	Whoever shall put away his wife GUILT OF ADULTERY	always irrelevant	GUILT OF ADULTERY except for the cause of fornication / always relevant		always adultery / ADULTERY causes her to commit adultery	ADULTERY and whoever shall marry her that is divorced commits adultery
Lu 16:18	never adultery	GUILT OF ADULTERY and marries another commits adultery	Whoever puts away his wife	always irrelevant	always relevant		always adultery	ADULTERY and whoever marries her that is put away from her husband commits adultery
Mt 19:9	never adultery	and shall marry another commits adultery GUILT OF ADULTERY	Whoever shall put away his wife	always irrelevant	GUILT OF ADULTERY except it be for fornication / always relevant		always adultery	ADULTERY and whoever marries her which is put away commits adultery
Mk 10:11	never adultery	GUILT OF ADULTERY and marry another commits adultery against her	Whoever shall put away his wife	always irrelevant	always relevant		always adultery	always adultery
Mk 10:12	never adultery	usually irrelevant		always irrelevant	always relevant	And if a woman shall put away her husband	GUILT OF ADULTERY and be married to another, she commits adultery	always adultery

Mt. 5:32. Whoever shall put away his wife.
Lu. 16:18. Whoever puts away his wife.
Mt. 19:9. Whoever shall put away his wife.
Mk. 10:11. Whoever shall put away his wife.

Four out of five cases Jesus presented about divorce are about a husband divorcing his wife, and only one out of five is about a wife divorcing her husband. The husband is the one responsible to hold the marriage together. "Therefore shall a man leave his father and his mother, and shall <u>cleave to his wife,</u> and they shall be one flesh," Gen. 2:24.

Mt. 5:32. Except for the cause of fornication.
Mt. 19:9. Except it be for fornication.
Deut. 24:1. Because he found some uncleanness in her.

If a husband divorces his wife because she committed fornication (which might be less than the actual act of adultery by becoming one flesh), then she bears the guilt of ending the one-flesh union with her x-husband when she becomes (or became) one flesh with another man.

Mt. 5:32. Causes her to commit adultery.

A husband who divorces a wife for any reason less than fornication, bears the guilt of causing her to have to commit adultery via remarriage to be married.

Lu. 16:18. And marries another commits adultery.
Mt. 19:9. And shall marry another commits adultery.
Mk. 10:11. And marry another commits adultery against her.
Ex. 21:10. If he take him another wife; her food, her raiment, and her duty of marriage, shall he not diminish; and if he do not these three unto her, then shall she go out free.

A husband who divorces his wife and thereby neglects her entirely and marries another, is even worse than a husband who adds an additional wife, and then neglects a preexisting wife. In both cases, he causes her to need to commit adultery at remarriage to receive her rightful food, clothing, and lovemaking to preserve her chastity per Exodus 21.

Mt. 5:32. And whoever shall marry her that is divorced commits adultery.
Mt. 19:9. And whoever marries her that is put away from her husband commits adultery.
Mk. 10:11. And whoever marries her which is put away commits adultery.

Jesus' scenarios assume an innocently divorced woman doesn't make love to anyone after her x-husband divorces her, until her second husband commits one act of adultery with her by breaking her one-flesh union with her x-husband by consummating her remarriage, even though the x-husband who wrongly divorced her will bear the guilt of their act of adultery. If a divorced woman does break her one-flesh union with her x-husband by making love to someone else before consummating her remarriage to her second husband, the second husband doesn't commit adultery, though he does break her one-flesh union with whatever man was with her before him.

Mk. 10:11. And if a woman shall put away her husband, and be married to another, she commits adultery.

A wife who divorces her husband and marries another, commits adultery by ending the one-flesh union with her x-husband when she becomes one flesh with her new husband at her remarriage. But, if she divorced him because he failed to provide food, clothing, and lovemaking, then her x-husband bears the guilt of that adultery.

Diagrams of Jesus' Teaching

The following diagrams Jesus' teachings on divorce and remarriage. Diagonal shading represents the wife's one-flesh union with her first husband; vertical shading represents her one-flesh union with her second husband; and thick-bordered boxes represent marriages. All Jesus' scenarios assume there is only one other man involved besides the first husband. If a woman has multiple one-flesh relationships before her remarriage, then the details of when each one-flesh relationship is broken, and of each sin of fornication vs. adultery, can be adjusted based on the same principles presented in these teachings.

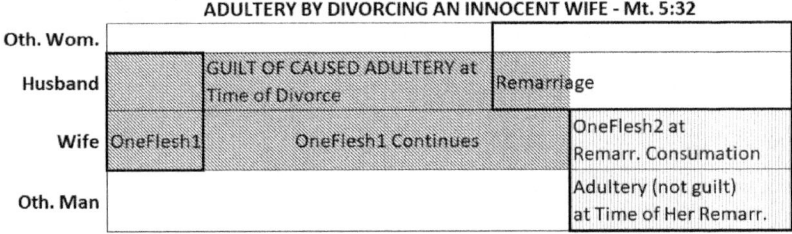

			ADULTERY BY DIVORCING AN INNOCENT WIFE - Mt. 5:32		
Oth. Wom.					
Husband		GUILT OF CAUSED ADULTERY at Time of Divorce		Remarriage	
Wife	OneFlesh1	OneFlesh1 Continues		OneFlesh2 at Remarr. Consumation	
Oth. Man				Adultery (not guilt) at Time of Her Remarr.	

Mt. 5:32. Whoever shall put away his wife, saving for the cause of fornication, causes her to commit adultery. And whoever shall marry her that is divorced commits adultery.

A husband who divorces a wife that didn't commit adultery, ends their marriage, but not their one-flesh union even when he remarries. Therefore, in addition to being cruel and hard-hearted, he also bears the guilt of causing her to have to commit adultery by breaking their one-flesh union by becoming one flesh with another man, if she wants to be a married woman, whether she ever remarries or not. A man who marries a divorced woman who wasn't divorced because of fornication, commits adultery by breaking the one flesh union between the divorced woman and her x-husband, but the husband that divorced her bears the guilt.

ADULTERY BY COMMITTING FORNICATION & BEING DIVORCED - Mt. 5:32; 19:9					
Oth. Wom.					
Husband			Divorce & Cruelty	Remarriage	
Wife	OneFlesh1	OneFlesh2 & GUILT OF ADULTERY at Time of Forn.			Remarriage
Oth. Man		GUILT OF ADULTERY at Time of Her Forn.			

A wife who commits fornication bears the guilt of breaking the one-flesh union with her husband by becoming one flesh with another man before or after the divorce, but the husband that divorces her is still guilty of cruelty, hardness of heart, and unforgiveness.

ADULTERY BY NEGLECTING AN INNOCENT WIFE - Mt. 19:9; Lu. 16:18; Mk. 10:11				
Oth. Wom.				
Husband		Divorce & Cruelty	GUILT OF ADULTERY BY NEGLECT at Time of Remarr.	
Wife	OneFlesh1	OneFlesh1 Continues		OneFlesh2 at Time of Remarr. Consum.
Oth. Man				Adultery (not guilt) at Time of Her Remarr.

Mt. 19:9. Whoever shall put away his wife, except it be for fornication, and shall marry another, commits adultery; and whoever marries her which is put away commits adultery.

Lu. 16:18. Whoever puts away his wife, and marries another, commits adultery; and whoever marries her that is put away from her husband commits adultery.

Mk. 10:11. Whoever shall put away his wife, and marry another, commits adultery against her.

A husband who divorces a wife that didn't commit adultery, ends their marriage but not their one-flesh union, even when he remarries. But divorcing and neglecting her, and then adding another wife, is even worse than adding another wife and then neglecting to provide his earlier wife's food, clothing, and lovemaking to safeguard her chastity. Therefore, in addition to being cruel and hard-hearted, he also bears the guilt of her adultery when she ends their one-flesh union by becoming one with another man at her remarriage or before. Yeshua wants us to know that a husband who divorces his wife for a lesser reason than fornication, violates Exodus 21, about protecting a wife's chastity by providing for her, in addition to Deuteronomy 24, about protecting a wife's chastity by not divorcing her.

ADULTERY BY DIVORCING A PROVIDING HUSBAND AND REMARRYING - Mk. 10:10-12

Oth. Wom.				
Husband			Remarriage	
Wife	OneFlesh1	Divorce OneFlesh1 Continues	OneFlesh2 & GUILT OF ADULTERY at Time of Remarriage Consummation	
Oth. Man			Adultery (not guilt) at Time of Her Remarriage	

Mk. 10:10-12. And if a woman shall put away her husband, and be married to another, she commits adultery.

A wife who divorces her husband, remains one flesh with him, even after the divorce ends their marriage, and even after her x-husband remarries. When she marries another, she bears the guilt of her own adultery by breaking her one-flesh union with her x-husband by becoming one flesh with her new husband.

However, the principle taught in Matthew 5:32 and the other divorce verses, is that the guilt of adultery is often put to the account of the person who caused the adultery, rather than the one who actually engaged in physical relations, and the same diagram as for "Adultery by Neglecting an Innocent Wife" above would apply, except the Divorce event would be moved to the wife's row. If the wife divorced her husband because he failed to provide food, clothing (including shelter, safety, etc.), and lovemaking, per Exodus 21:10, then her x-husband bears the guilt per Exodus 21:11. Also, a wife who divorces a husband is not guilty of the cruelty that a husband who divorces a wife is guilty of (see the next section on "Remarriage").

A husband who has physical relations with a woman other than his wife, commits fornication or adultery, depending on the marital status of the woman, and becomes one flesh with her, but he doesn't thereby break the one-flesh union with his wife or stop being one flesh with her. Though a husband who divorces his wife because of her sexual "uncleanness," Deut. 24:1, doesn't thereby become guilty of causing her to commit adultery; a wife who divorces her providing husband because of his sexual sin is still guilty of adultery when she ends their one-flesh union by becoming one with another by remarrying, because only neglect permits her to divorce her husband per Exodus 21.

In other words, the diagram for a wife that divorces her husband because of his sexual sin and then remarries, is the same as the diagram for a wife that divorces a husband for any other reason besides Exodus 21. A husband's sexual sin is still sin, and it's cruel to his wife, but it doesn't directly affect her chastity.

1 Cor 7. Remarriage

1-9. Most Unmarried People Are Required to Marry

1 Cor. 7:1-2. Now concerning the things whereof you wrote to me, it's good for a man not to touch a woman. Nevertheless, to avoid fornication, let **every man** *have his own wife, and let* **every woman** *have her own husband.*

The Corinthians had asked Paul if widows should remarry. Paul expanded his answer to address all celibacy and marriage. He said celibacy is good, but most people are required to marry to avoid fornication. "Every man" and "every woman" includes divorced men and women. They have just as much obligation to marry to avoid fornication as everyone else. "Remarriage" is just called "marriage" in the Bible.

Also, as detailed earlier, when Paul says "let every man have his own [heautou] wife," it refers to "his own" reflexively and exclusively; whereas when he says "let every woman have her own [idios] husband," it refers to "her own" that pertains to her, but may pertain to others also, because of polygyny.

The Bible refers to divorced women several times. For the high priest, "a widow, or a divorced woman, or profane, or a harlot, these he shall not take," Lev. 21:14. Divorced women are also mentioned in Lev. 21:7, 22:13, Num. 30:9, Ez. 44:22, Mt. 5:32, Mt. 19:9, and Lu. 16:18. But the Bible never refers to a "divorced man." It would be senseless and irrelevant. Only the marital statuses of women are relevant. Also, when a man is divorced, he might still be married to other wives, whereas a woman is always unmarried when she's divorced. So it's not a useful term for men.

1 Cor. 7:3-5. Let the husband render to the wife due benevolence, and likewise also the wife to the husband. The wife doesn't have power of her own body, but the husband, and likewise also the husband doesn't have power of his own body, but the wife. Don't defraud one the other, except it be with consent for a time, so that you may give yourselves to fasting and prayer; and come together again, so that Satan doesn't tempt you for your incontinency.

Physical relations outside of marriage are sin; but abstention within marriage is sin.

1 Cor. 7:6-7a. But I speak this by permission, and not of commandment. For I wish that all men were even as I myself. But every man has his proper gift of God, one after this manner, and another after that.

Paul <u>permits</u> "for a man not to touch a woman," vs. 1, by remaining single "even as I myself," vs. 7a. But he <u>commands</u> marriage for those who need to marry to avoid fornication. Though Paul had been a rabbi, his permission of celibacy is in contradiction to Rabbinic Judaism that requires all men to marry.

"Every man is obligated to marry a woman in order to be fruitful, and to multiply and anyone who doesn't engage in being fruitful and multiplying is as if he spills blood, ... and causes the divine presence to depart from Israel. ... He who does not marry is not allowed to make a blessing or to engage in Torah etc. and he is not called a man. ... It is incumbent on every man that they should marry a woman at the age of 18 and the diligent get married at 13, ... and he who lets 20 years pass, or he who does not want to marry, the courts can force him to marry in order to fulfill the mitzvah of being fruitful," Shulchan Aruch, Even HaEzer, 1:3 (also Talmud, Yevamot 63b). The rabbis based their requirement to marry on God's command to Adam and Eve to "be fruitful and multiply," Gen. 1:28, but their interpretation is incorrect, because the command would have been repeated in the Law if it applied to every man individually during Moses' time.

1 Cor. 7:8-9. I say therefore to the unmarried [masculine, i.e. both men and women] and widows [feminine], it is good for them [masculine, both men and women] if they remain even as I. But if they can't contain, let them marry, for it is better to marry than to burn [with lust].

Paul sums up this section by saying it's preferable for unmarried people, including the widows they specifically asked about, to stay unmarried, but only if they're strong enough to avoid fornication without marriage. Some interpret the word "unmarried" here to mean "widowers," because the noun is masculine in Greek, and to make it parallel the word "widows." But the concept of a 'widower', is never found in the Bible, because only the marital statuses of women are ever relevant.

"Unmarried" is masculine because it includes all unmarried men, as well as divorced and virgin women, and a group with any males uses a masculine noun. Widows are broken out separately because the original question to Paul had been, "Should widows remarry?" Divorced women are called "unmarried," in verse 10, "Let not the wife depart from her husband. But and if she depart, let her remain unmarried." And virgin women are called "unmarried" in verse 34, "There is difference also between a wife and a virgin. The unmarried woman cares for the things of the Lord." Virgin women are also dealt with separately in a later section because of their unique situation, including the woman's father being included in the decision making. Virgin status has no relevance for men.

Verses 8-9 require all unmarried persons who "cannot contain," to marry. Unlike the concerns of pastors today because of their gender-equal, culturally-determined misinterpretations of scripture, there's no qualifying clauses for divorced persons, or concerns about who divorced whom, or the reasons for the divorce, or the innocent or guilty party, or the validity of the divorce, since all divorces are valid. If Paul wanted to forbid remarriage to divorced people, or to some subset of divorced people, this would've been the place to say so. Since Paul doesn't say otherwise, we should assume all "unmarried," 1 Cor. 7:8, including divorced people, have the responsibility to marry to avoid fornication.

10-24. Married People Are Required to Stay Married

1 Cor. 7:10-11. And to the married I command, yet not I, but the Lord, "Let not the wife depart from her husband." But and if she depart, let her remain unmarried or be reconciled to her husband, and let not the husband put away his wife.

Paul says, "I command, yet not I but the Lord," because Yeshua had already given commands regarding married persons in the gospels. Jesus said divorce is never right, and Paul's advice harmonizes with that. "Let not the wife depart from her husband, ... and let not the husband put away his wife," 1 Cor. 7:10-11. No exception clauses are needed.

Paul said a wife who divorces her husband should

"remain unmarried or be reconciled to her husband." Why didn't he also say a husband who divorces his wife should "remain unmarried or be reconciled to his wife?" First, if a husband had more than one wife at the time of the divorce, he won't be "unmarried" after a divorce, whereas a wife will always be unmarried after a divorce. Secondly, when a wife divorces her husband, biblically even her x-husband's remarriage doesn't prohibit her from returning to him, though practically today it does because of wrong teaching in society, whereas even biblically a wife's remarriage would prevent a husband from being able to remarry her.

Thirdly, there's more chance of an x-wife's x-husband accepting her back if she divorced him, than if he divorced her. But if reconciliation is unlikely, the unmarried still need to remarry to avoid fornication. Paul advised younger widows to remarry to avoid fornication, so he would probably advise younger divorced women to do the same. "Let not a widow be taken into the number under threescore years old, ... but the younger widows refuse, for when they have begun to wax wanton against Messiah they will marry. ... I will therefore that the younger women [virgins, divorced, and widows] marry [and] bear children," 1 Tim. 5:9-15.

Fourthly, if the x-husband won't provide food, clothing, safety, and lovemaking to his x-wife, she shouldn't return to him, even if he wants her to, and the guilt of her adultery at remarriage will be laid to his account. A godly woman may fight hard to keep her marriage before divorce, but afterwards it's sometimes wisest for her to look at the divorce as freedom from an oppressive marriage, rather than be too quick to reconcile.

Once a woman's chastity is violated by her becoming one flesh with a second husband at remarriage, subsequent lovemaking with him no longer violates her chastity. From that time on, the second husband is the one to whom Romans 7:1-4 now applies, and now someone will be guilty of adultery if she has physical relations with anyone but him as long as he lives.

To divorce her second husband and go back to her first husband would be adultery, "her former husband ... may not take her again," Deut. 24:1-4. Once a person remarries, it's just as wrong to end that marriage as for a previous marriage. Some believers, in deference to their teachers, build their lives around avoiding remarriage, and instead live lives of lust and recurring fornication instead. "Marriage is honorable in all, and the bed undefiled: but whoremongers and adulterers God will judge," Heb. 13:4.

Some relationships require a man and woman to cease physical relations rather than to marry. The Corinthian church condoned "fornication such as is not so much as named among Gentiles, that one should have his his stepmother," 1 Cor. 5:1. The Law forbids that relationship. "The nakedness of your father's wife shall you not uncover; it is your father's nakedness," Lev. 18:8. Paul commanded the Corinthian church to disassociate themselves from that man. "I have written to you not to keep company with anyone named a brother, who is sexually immoral, ... not even to eat with such a person. ... Put away from yourselves the evil person," 1 Cor. 5:11-12.

The Corinthian Church followed Paul's advice and the man repented, so Paul urged them to welcome him back. "This punishment which was inflicted by the majority is sufficient for such a man, so that, on the contrary, you ought rather to forgive and comfort him," 2 Cor. 2:6-7. Polygamy and remarriage were certainly more frequent in the early church, than incest with a stepmother, but you never hear Paul telling the church to disassociate themselves from any polygamous or remarried people, which he would have commanded, if it was adultery for them to remain married.

1 Cor. 7:12-16. But to the rest I speak, not the Lord. If any brother has a wife that doesn't believe, and she is pleased to dwell with him, let him not put her away. And the woman which has a husband that doesn't believe, and if he is pleased to dwell with her, let her not leave him. ... But if the unbelieving depart, let him depart. A brother or a sister is not under bondage in such cases, but God has called us to peace. For what do you know, O wife, whether you will save your husband? Or how do you know, O man, whether you will save your wife?

Yeshua hadn't covered the case of a believer being married to an unbeliever, but the advice is the same. Don't divorce your spouse, but you can't prevent your spouse from divorcing you. An unbelieving husband who divorces his believing wife will bear the guilt of her adultery when she remarries; and an unbelieving wife who divorces her believing husband will bear the guilt of her own adultery when she remarries. There is no adultery when a husband remarries, but he will thereby become guilty for his x-wife's having to remarry if he divorced her, as discussed before. Biblically, a believing husband would never divorce his wife, believer or not, though today he may sometimes have to since our society doesn't accept polygyny. A believing wife may sometimes have to divorce a husband, not for being an unbeliever, but for not providing for her per Exodus 21:10.

1 Cor. 7:17-24. But as God has distributed to every man, as the Lord has called every one, so let him walk. And so ordain I in all churches. ... Let every man abide in the same calling wherein he was called. Are you called being a servant? Care not for it. But if you may be made free, use it rather.

If the unbelieving spouse is willing to stay married, then don't divorce them because they're unbelievers, though all the other passages about divorce, like Exodus 21, still apply.

25-38. Virgin Women Are Free to Choose
1 Cor. 7:25. Now concerning virgins [feminine] I have no commandment of the Lord, yet I give my judgment, as one that has obtained mercy of the Lord to be faithful.

Yeshua gave no explicit commandment about virgin women in the gospels.

1 Cor. 7:26-32a. I suppose therefore that this is good for the present distress, I say, that it is good for a man to be so [single]. Are you bound to a wife? Seek not to be loosed. Are you freed from a wife? Seek not a wife. But and if you marry, you have not sinned; and if a virgin marry, she has not sinned. Nevertheless, such shall have trouble in the flesh; but I spare you. But this I say, brethren, the time is short. It remains, that both they that have wives will be as though they had none, ... for the fashion of this world passes away. But I would have you without being full of care [by being married].

Married people have to stay married, but single people have a choice. They aren't wrong to choose marriage, though marriage results in more hardship. If they want to stay single, but worry about missing out on experiencing the joys of marriage, they can remember life is like "a vapor that appears for a little time and then vanishes away," Jam. 4:14, and then, "they that have wives will be as though they had none," vs. 29, and there's no marriage after resurrection and glorification.

1 Cor. 7:32b-35. He that is unmarried cares for the things that belong to the Lord, how he may please the Lord; but he that is married cares for the things that are of the world, how he may please his wife. There is difference also between a wife and a virgin. The unmarried woman cares for the things of the Lord, that she may be holy both in body and in spirit; but she that is married cares for the things of the world, how she may please her husband. And this I speak for your own profit; not that I may cast a snare on you, but for that which is comely, and that you may attend on the Lord without distraction.

Paul says a person can accomplish more for the Lord as a single person. But he doesn't want to "cast a snare," vs. 35, to make a single person feel pressured to stay single so they can do more for the Lord, because most people need to marry to avoid fornication, and for their natural needs for companionship and help, etc. A person who should marry, but stayed single, would end up doing less for the Lord than if he married, because searching for substitutes for companionship would distract him, and fornication might destroy him.

1 Cor. 7:36-38. But if any man think that he behaves himself uncomely toward his virgin [daughter], if she pass the flower of her age, and need so require, let him do what he will, he sins not, let them marry. Nevertheless he that stands steadfast in his heart, having no necessity, but has power over his own will, and has so decreed in his heart that he will keep his virgin [daughter], does well. So then he that gives her in marriage does well; but he that doesn't give her in marriage does better.

Who would have a young woman's best interests in mind more than her own father, assuming he's a good father? Her father is less likely to be deceived by suiters who act loving to get what they're after, but are actually selfish. A good father wouldn't make any choices about his daughter's future without involving her in the decisions. He would want to help her achieve what is best for her. Biblically, engagement is as binding as marriage; but in our days, people don't intend it to be as binding as marriage when they get engaged, so it's not; and therefore, people today shouldn't go through with a marriage just because they're engaged.

1 Cor. 7:39-40. The wife is bound by the law as long as her husband lives, but if her husband is dead, she is at liberty to be married to whom she will, only in the Lord. But she is happier if she so abide, after my judgment; and I think also that I have the Spirit of God.

Paul finishes up by repeating his answer to the original question the Corinthians had asked, "should widows remarry?" He said widows are "at liberty," vs. 39, to remarry, but would probably be happier if they don't, if they don't need to to avoid fornication.

Like Romans 7:1-2, this verse shows the New Testament continues the Old Testament definition of adultery. Both the Old and New Testaments define chastity as a woman having physical relations with only one man as long as he lives, but not symmetrically as a man having physical relations with only one woman as long as she lives. The New Testament never says anything like the inverse of 1 Corinthians 7:39, "the husband is bound by the law as long as his wife lives; but if his wife is dead, he is at liberty to be married to whom he will."

It's relevant whether a wife's husband is still living, "as long as her husband lives," vs. 39, as to whether she can marry another. But it's irrelevant whether a husband's wife is still living as to whether he can marry another. And Paul dealt with the issue about widows remarrying, but not about 'widowers' remarrying, because that term is irrelevant in itself.

Culturally-dominated Bible teachers assume gender-specific verses like this can be freely reversed because they've allowed our modern culture to influence their interpretation of scripture, and because they don't understand the goodness of inequality in authority structures.

Additional Considerations about Polygamy

Eph 5:21-6:9. Why Only Men Can Have Multiple Spouses

Ephesians 5:21-6:9. "[ALL:] Submitting yourselves one to another in the fear of God [but in different ways appropriate to your office]. [HUSBAND/WIFE RELATIONSHIP:] Wives, submit yourselves unto your own husbands, as unto the Lord. ... Husbands, love your wives, even as Messiah also loved the church, and gave himself for it. ... [PARENT/CHILD RELATIONSHIP:] Children, obey your parents in the Lord: for this is right. ... And, you fathers, provoke not your children to wrath: but bring them up in the nurture and admonition of the Lord. [MASTER/ SERVANT RELATIONSHIP:] Servants, be obedient to them that are your masters according to the flesh. ... And, you masters, do the same things unto them, forbearing threatening: knowing that your Master also is in heaven."

There are three parallel superior/inferior relationships listed in this passage; not superior/inferior in value, but in position and role: The Husband/Wife Relationship, the Parent/Child Relationship, and the Master/Servant Relationship. These same three relationships are repeated in the same order in Colossians 3:14-4:1.

"[ALL] Above all these things put on charity [but in different ways appropriate to your office]. ... [HUSBAND/WIFE RELATIONSHIP:] Wives, submit to your own husbands. ... Husbands, love your wives and do not be bitter toward them. [PARENT/CHILD RELATIONSHIP:] Children, obey your parents in all things. ... Fathers, do not provoke your children, lest they become discouraged. [MASTER/SERVANT RELATIONSHIP:] Bondservants, obey in all things your masters according to the flesh. ... Masters, give your bondservants what is just and fair."

In all three relationships, the inferior position is mentioned first, and the superior position is mentioned second. In all three relationships, there can only be one person in the superior role, but there can be multiple persons in the inferior role. A father can have more than one child, but each child can have only one father; a master can have more than one servant, but each servant can have only one master; and a husband can have more than one wife, but each wife can have only one husband.

The reason there can be only one person in the superior role of each relationship is that, as Yeshua said, "no man can serve two masters," Mt. 6:24. A loving leader will lead in a participatory rather than an authoritarian manner, since his goal is the welfare of those he leads, but to join the people together, only one person can have rightful authority. "Can two walk together except they are agreed?" Amos 3:3. If people walking together make their own decisions on which direction to go, they will end up walking alone.

A body can have more than one member, but it can have only one head. "He is the head of the body, the church," Col. 1:18; "Now you are the body of Messiah, and members individually," 1 Cor. 12:27. And a husband can have more than one wife, but a wife can only have one husband.

"For the husband is head of the wife, as also Messiah is head of the church, and he is the savior of the body."

If Messiah can be one flesh with more than one believer at the same time, then a husband can be one flesh with more than one wife at the same time. "For we are members of His body, of His flesh and of His bones. For this cause shall a man leave his father and mother, and shall be joined unto his wife, and they two shall be one flesh," Eph. 5:23-30.

These verses in Ephesians quote Genesis, "Therefore shall a man leave his father and his mother, and shall cleave unto his wife: and they shall be one flesh," Gen. 2:24. No one in the Old Testament thought the "one flesh" of Genesis 2:24 taught against polygamy. The verse was written by Moses, a polygamist, and he should understand what he meant by it better than modernists today.

A husband can be one flesh with more than one wife at the same time, just as God is one with more than one of us at a time. You are one with God because you are in him and he is in you, and I am one with God because I am in him and he is in me. My being one with God does not hinder your also being one with God. "That they all may be one; as you, Father, are in me, and I in you, that they also may be one in us: that the world may believe that you have sent me," Jn. 17:21. One wife being one flesh with a husband does not hinder another wife from being one flesh with the same husband.

Some people claim the Bible prohibits polygamy because God created only one wife for Adam. But how many wives should he have created for Adam if he wanted to show that polygamy is permitted, though not recommended? If he created two wives for Adam, men would think God requires men to marry exactly two wives, and that only one is not permitted. God created the perfect number of wives for Adam to show that monogamy is preferred, but polygamy is permitted.

Also, God had other concerns in creating Eve than to illustrate the number of wives a man is permitted to have. It's important that we're all descended from one man and one woman, to demonstrate the brotherhood of men, and so all men can be saved through one second Adam, for example. Even scientifically, mitochondrial DNA, the Eve gene, shows we're all descended from one created human couple, not from various gradual evolutionary sources. It wasn't necessary for God to create two wives for Adam to show us he allows polygamy, because he told us so through the definition of adultery and the examples of the great men of God throughout the Bible.

Some people say the use of the definite article "the" and the singular noun "wife," as in "the husband is the head of the wife," Eph. 5:23, proves God's will is for monogamy only. But the previous verse, Eph. 5:22, says "Wives, submit yourselves unto your own husbands." Does that mean marriage must be polyamorous? Phrases like "the woman" and "the man" in passages like "for as the woman [Eve] is of the man [Adam], even so is the man [all men except Adam] also by the woman," 1 Cor. 11:12, mean all men are born of women, but says nothing about the number of male children each woman may have.

Matthew 10:24, "the disciple is not above his master, nor the servant above his lord," doesn't mean Jesus had only one disciple and masters only ever have one servant. "The servant abides not in the house forever," Jn. 8:35, doesn't mean each household can have only one servant. "The branch cannot bear fruit of itself, except it abide in the vine," Jn. 15:4, doesn't mean vines can only have one branch. "The brother shall deliver up the brother to death, and the father the child," Mt. 10:21, doesn't mean brothers can have only one brother, or fathers can have only one child.

If God had said, "Let each husband love his wives," instead of "husbands, love your wives,"

Eph. 5:25; Col. 3:19, men would wrongly interpret it to mean God requires, rather than permits, polygamy. He could have said, "Let each husband love his wife, or wives, if circumstances result in his having more than one wife," but that would under-emphasize each husband's one-on-one, unique relationship with each wife. The man who had a thousand wives said, "There are threescore queens, and fourscore concubines, and virgins without number. My dove, my undefiled is but one; she is the only one of her mother, she is the choice one of her that bare her. The daughters saw her, and blessed her," Song 6:8-9.

Do Polygamous Families Have More Trouble?

Some people say polygamous families in the Bible have so many problems it proves polygamy is against God's will. They say look at the rivalry between Sarah and Hagar, between Rachel and Leah, and between Hannah and Peninnah. Polygamy does create some unique challenges. "Rachel said, 'With great wrestling have I wrestled with my sister,'" Gen. 30:8. But most of the trouble in polygamous families comes from being families, not from being polygamous. Family life is usually messy.

It seems like polygamous families in the Bible

have more trouble because, for the most part, they are the only ones we have much information about. It's like how Bible teachers usually portray the church of Corinth as the worst of all the churches because of the problems mentioned in 1st and 2nd Corinthians, but the Corinthian church is the only one whose meetings we get to sit in on. It would have been inappropriate for Paul to have aired the dirty laundry of the church of Rome in his letter to them about systematic theology, or of the church in Ephesus in his letter to them about the mystery of Jews and Gentiles comprising one body in Messiah in heavenly places.

There's one monogamous family we know a lot about, that of Isaac and Rebekah; and the Bible mentions more problems for them than for any other family. Isaac showed favoritism towards Esau, and not for good reasons. "Isaac loved Esau, because he did eat of his venison, but Rebekah loved Jacob," Gen. 25:28. Rebekah helped Jacob trick Isaac into blessing him instead of Esau, and when Esau found out, he decided to kill Jacob. Jacob fled to Haran, and probably never saw his mother again during this lifetime. When Jacob returned to Canaan about twenty years later, he split his family into two groups, so "if Esau come to the one company and smite it then the other company which is left shall escape," Gen. 32:8.

Some people say polygamy results in child brides and imprisoned women, and sometimes, especially in cults, it does. We've all heard of teenage girls who were forced to marry cult leaders and prevented from escaping to the outside world. But it's the forced marriages and imprisonment that are wrong and should be litigated against, whether in monogamy or polygamy, and not polygamy itself. Both polygamy and monogamy are subject to abuse.

Is it really better for single mothers to be forced to raise their children alone because the law forbids them to marry a man who already has another wife? Under polygamy, all women who want to be married, can be married. And under polygamy, all women are free to marry the best of men, not the leftovers. Wars and a shorter life span for men always ensures there's more women than men available.

But even more significantly, not all men are marriageable material. Women should have the option to skip over the crass, selfish, immature men, who are still children in men's bodies, and be able to marry a man who will love and care for them. With polygamy (actually polygyny), women are free to pick any man, even if he's already married; whereas men can only choose from among the single women.

Also, when women have access to men who will commit to and marry them via polygamy, the other men will also have to become willing to commit and marry in order to compete for the women. Godly polygamous marriage reduces the opportunities for men in society to enjoy women physically without getting married, and then move on to another woman whenever they feel like it.

It's tragic that women often blame themselves for suffering which other people put on them. They are like abused children that need to understand that not all parents are good, and in abusive situations, it's not the fault of the abused.

"I Need to Be in Love," by the Carpenters
The hardest thing I've ever done
Is keep believing
There's someone in this crazy world for me ...

I used to say, no promises
Let's keep it simple
But freedom only helps you say goodbye ...

I know I need to be in love
I know I've wasted too much time
I know I ask perfection of a quite imperfect world
And fool enough to think that's what I'll find

So here I am with pockets full of good intentions
But none of them will comfort me tonight

I'm wide awake at four a.m.
Without a friend in sight

No, Karen Carpenter, it's not your fault you're alone. It's not because you're expecting "perfection of a quite imperfect world." Your expectations are not unrealistically high. The problem is that society has been teaching men to be selfish and uncommitted, and it won't allow women to become second wives to the ever-shrinking supply of unselfish and committed men.

On the other hand, for a wife, it's better to be her husband's only wife, and have all his attention. An additional wife is a rival, which is why sisters aren't to be put in that position. "You shall not take a wife to her sister, to be a rival to her, to uncover her nakedness, besides the other in her life-time," Lev. 18:18. Thus we see the competition between Leah and Rachel in Genesis 30, including "Rachel said, 'With mighty wrestlings have I wrestled with my sister'" (Gen. 30:8). So although polygyny isn't adultery, fornication, unchastity, or any kind of sin in itself, failing to love is sin, and it's usually unloving to an existing wife to add another, though sometimes circumstances warrant otherwise.

Jewish marriage contracts often included promises not to add a second wife in Sephardic communities where polygyny was not entirely forbidden by Ashkenazi rabbis around 1000 AD. "Istanbul custom dictated that the marriage contract must contain the husband's sworn promise ... not to take another woman as a second wife," A History of the Jewish Community in Istanbul; Minna Rozen; page 167. "In Africa, where Mohammedan influence was strongest, the custom was to include in the marriage contract the following paragraph: 'The said bridegroom ... hereby promises that he will not take a second wife during the lifetime of said bride ... except with her consent," The Jewish Encyclopedia; Isadore Singer, Managing Editor; Volume X, page 121.

The Source of the Monogamy-Only Doctrine

We've seen the Bible doesn't condemn polygamy, so where does society's "monogamy only" doctrine come from? The Western culture of the Greeks and Romans prohibited polygamy centuries before Christianity. Only after the Roman emperor Constantine put a Christian veneer on the pagan religion of Rome, and required everyone to follow the resulting Roman Catholic Church, did so-called 'Christianity' begin prohibiting polygamy.

Columnist Michael E. Price posted an article on the Psychology Today website on Sep 09, 2011, entitled "Why We Think Monogamy Is Normal." He said, "Monogamy's spread in the West had something to do with the influence of Christianity, but not as much as you might expect. ... Socially imposed monogamy was first established in ancient Greece and Rome, centuries before Christianity even existed."

One of the big moral deficiencies of the "monogamy only" doctrine (or SIM, "Socially Imposed Monogamy," as the literature calls it), is that it always becomes "serial monogamy" in practice in societies. Serial monogamy is like polygamy in that men marry more than one wife; but unlike polygamy, in that the men divorce and remarry one wife after another, rather than continuing to provide and care for their earlier wives. There's an economic study called, "From Polygyny to Serial Monogamy," by David de la Croix and Fabio Mariani, 2015, in Review of Economic Studies, that shows there are even economic reasons for this progression in monogamous societies.

In "The History and Philosophy of Marriage," by James Campbell, 1869, he says, "The monogamy of the ancient Romans ... did not require their marriages to be permanent. Seduction, adultery, and whoredom were rather the rule than the exception among them; but marriage was for other and more important purposes than those of love. ... If a man could, at any time, form a new alliance which would give him more wealth or influence, he always felt himself at liberty to divorce his wife, and form that new alliance. ... Such were the frequency of their divorces, and the intricacy of their relationships caused by their numerous adoptions, that it has been almost impossible for the best historians and biographers to give us any intelligible account of their families." Campbell then went on to provide a sample of Roman monogamy via the six emperors of the Julio-Claudian dynasty.

46 BC Julius Caesar

Julius Caesar married a succession of four wives. He upgraded from his wealthy first wife, Cossutia, to marry Pompeia as soon as he attained some political influence at age eighteen. He divorced Pompeia because Marc Antony's son, Clodius, snuck into his home dressed as a woman to seduce her during a women's only religious event being held there. But as for Caesar himself, Suetonius says he committed adultery with many of the highest-ranking ladies in Rome, including Posthumia the wife of Servius Sulpitius, Lollia the wife of Aulus Gabinius, Tertullia the wife of Marcus Crassus, Mutia the wife of Pompey the

Great, Eunoe the wife of Bogudes, Cleopatra Queen of Egypt, Servilia the mother of Marcus Brutus, and her daughter Tertia.

27 BC Augustus

Augustus was the son of Attia, the daughter of Julia, the sister of Julius Caesar. He became emperor by defeating Pompey and Marc Antony after the assassination of Julius Caesar. He married a succession of four women. He divorced his third wife, Scribonia, on the day she gave birth to his only legitimate child, Julia; and he obtained his fourth wife, Livia, by making her husband, Tiberius Claudius, divorce her, even though she had borne Claudius two sons, including the next emperor, Tiberius, and was pregnant with his third child.

Augustus made his general, Agrippa, divorce his wife and marry Augustus' niece Marcella. Then after Marcella's brother Marcellus died, who was married to Augustus' daughter Julia; Augustus made Agrippa divorce his niece Marcella and marry his daughter Julia. After Agrippa himself died, Augustus made his stepson Tiberius divorce Agrippa's daughter Vipsania and marry Julia. (Hey, at least there's no polygamy involved, right?)

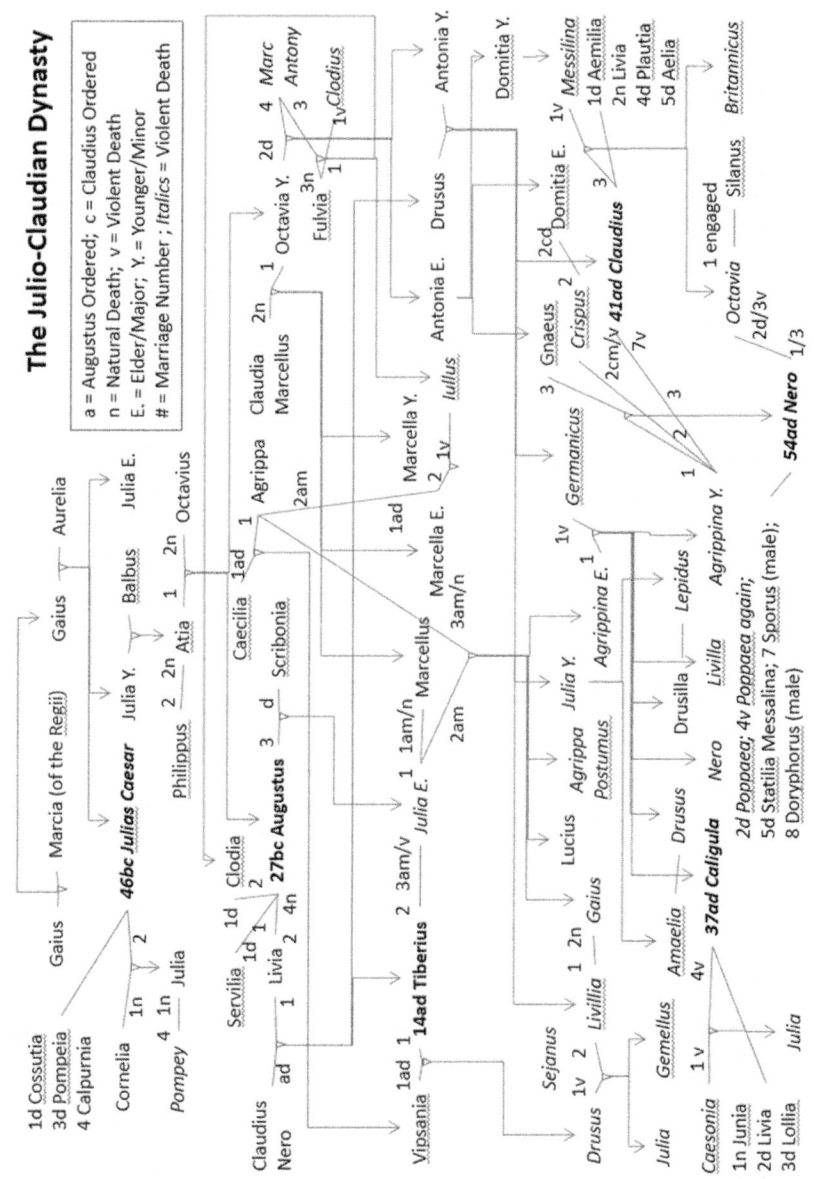

The Julio-Claudian Dynasty

Augustus' daughter Julia herself was so dissolute that eventually Augustus made Tiberius divorce her, and banished her to the island of Pandateria. Marc Antony's son, Iullus, was executed as one of her lovers at that time. Augustus constantly employed men to pimp both married and unmarried noble women for him. He reportedly once took the wife of a dinner guest from beside her husband, raped her, and returned her visibly shaken before the meal was over.

14 AD Tiberius

Tiberius was of the Claudian family mentioned earlier, and not related by blood to Augustus, but he was his stepson (via his mother Livia, Augustus' wife), his son-in-law (via his wife Julia, Augustus' daughter), and his adopted son. The first thing Tiberius did when he came to power was to murder his wife Julia's son, Agrippa Posthumus, because Agrippa Posthumus was also an adopted son of Augustus.

Tiberius spent the last ten years of his twenty-three-year reign on the pleasure island of Capri where he lived in all manner of indescribable sexual uncleanness. While he was living at Capri, the head of his Praetorian Guard, Sejanus, who was the lover of Livilla, the wife of Tiberias' son Drusus, managed to get Drusus and others relatives of Tiberius murdered. Later, Tiberias retaliated and had Sejanus, Livilla, and the remainder of Julia's children killed, including the famous Agrippina, and Julia the Younger, as well as many other nobility in a purge.

37 AD Caligula

Caligula, one of Julia's grandsons, was spared during Tiberias' purge, and spent the last six years of Tiberius' life living with him on Capri. He married a series of four women. He also made his sister Drusilla's husband divorce her so he could live with her in incest. She died less than a year later, so he built a temple for her worship, and lived in incest with his other two sisters, Livilla and Agrippina, whom he also prostituted to his favorite male lovers.

Caligula obtained his second wife, Livia, by snatching her from her wedding he had been invited to. He divorced her three days later, but would not let her return to her fiancé. He obtained his third wife, Lollia, by ordering her husband, who was away with her in a foreign province, to divorce her and send her to him in Rome, because he had heard people extol the beauty of her grandmother. He divorced her a year later to marry his pregnant mistress, Caesonia, who already had three illegitimate children from others.

Caligula held feasts for high ranking men and their wives, and would pick one of them to be sent to his bedroom at the end of the meal. He also opened a brothel in the palace to supplement the royal income and forced high-ranking, married and single, noble women to serve in it as prostitutes. After only four years of rule, he and his family were assassinated.

41 AD Claudius

Claudius was Caligula's uncle. He married six times. When he became emperor, he divorced his fourth wife to marry his pregnant mistress, Messalina, who has been called the Roman Jezebel for her lust and cruelty. She committed adultery with many chief officers, and forced many respectable married women to prostitute themselves. Eventually, she plotted with one of her lovers to kill Claudius, and was discovered and executed.

Next Claudius forced the senate to legalize marriages between uncles and nieces so he could marry his niece Agrippina the Younger. Agrippina then made the fiancé of Claudius' daughter Octavia divorce her, so she could marry Octavia to her own son Nero, from a previous marriage, to Gnaeus. Agrippina also got Claudius to adopt Nero, and then poisoned Claudius, making her son Nero emperor.

54 AD Nero

After Nero became emperor, he developed a passion for an Asian freed-woman named Acte. Agrippina thought this might weaken her motherly influence, so she threatened her son

Nero, that if didn't stop seeing Acte, she would use her influence as daughter of the beloved general Germanicus, to have the army put Claudius' son Britannicus into power. Instead, Nero had Britannicus poisoned.

Next Nero became infatuated with Poppaea, whose husband was away as governor of Portugal. Agrippina complained so much about this new threat to her motherly influence that Nero decided to have his mother killed. First, he sent her to sea in a ship that was designed to fall apart, but she survived the shipwreck. Then he sent assassins to her apartment who killed her.

Nero then divorced Octavia and married Poppaea, but he feared the complaints of the people so much that he divorced Poppaea and married Octavia again. After obtaining false witnesses that Octavia had committed adultery, he divorced her again, and had her banished to the island of Pandateria, where he had her killed and her head sent to Poppaea. He married Poppaea again, who bore him his only child, a daughter, who lived only lived a few months.

The following year Nero, it is suspected, burned Rome, with great loss of life in the narrow streets and fast-spreading flames, and then blamed the fire on the Christians, and began a horrible persecution of them. Poppaea died when Nero kicked her in the stomach in a fit of rage while she was in a late stage of pregnancy. Nero then had the husband of Statilia Messilina killed so he could marry her. He soon divorced her, and successively married two men. He committed suicide after ruling for fourteen years, and the Julio-Claudian dynasty (thankfully) came to an end.

So which was godlier, the monogamy of the Roman Emperors, or the polygamy of the Israelite kings? Israel's law required a man to 'add' a second wife, if need be, rather than divorce a pre-existing wife. You might think the modern prohibition against polygamy comes from Jesus' teaching about divorce, but modern Bible teachers would not be so quick to interpret Jesus' words as prohibiting polygamy if they weren't already indoctrinated by two thousand years of Roman culture.

There are hundreds of references in the Shulchan Aruch about levirate marriage, inheritance, etc. for when a man has multiple wives. "A man can marry many women, even 100, whether all at once or one after another, and his wife cannot prevent [it], as long as he can give the appropriate [amount of] food, clothing and "time" (marital relations) to each one, and he can't force them to live in one courtyard, rather each one for herself. ... The rabbis commanded that a person shouldn't marry more than 4 wives, even if he has a lot of money, so that they get their "time" [at least] once a month," Shulchan Aruch, Ever HaEzer 76:7. However, around 1000 AD, Rabbi Gershom prohibited polygamy, and the Ashkenazi Jews follow his prohibition; while the Sephardic Jews don't. Why? Because the Ashkenazi Jews lived in European areas where polygamy was illegal and Sephardic Jews lived in Muslim areas where it wasn't illegal. So the rabbis, like the majority of Christian Bible teachers, let the dominant culture change their perspective of the Bible, instead of letting the Bible change our culture.

Single mother households are plentiful in the West because Western societies see nothing wrong with a man maintaining physical relations with an unlimited number of women so long as he doesn't commit to them and provide for them as if they're married. The world hates polygyny, because it hates patriarchy and authority. It's part of the "mystery of lawlessness," 2 Thess. 2:7 ASV, at work in preparation for the coming world-dictatorship of the anti-Messiah.

Practical Considerations About Polygamy

Just because polygamy isn't immoral, doesn't

mean it's practical. Sinful men like us can't adequately care for one even woman to the extent each deserves. There are significant challenges for anyone who thinks their situation might call for a polygamous solution. Godly Christians are available online to help new polygynous families.

Just because the Bible permits polygamy doesn't mean people can ignore the cultural and legal risks. "We ought to obey God rather than men," Acts 5:29; but we should also be "wise as serpents, harmless as doves," Mt. 10:16. If you marry a second wife to protect and provide for her and to maintain her chastity, as the Bible dictates, and you end up in jail because of it, then you end up harming even your first wife. If a couple in China breaks the law to try to save their child from a state-ordered abortion, the Bible supports their decision. But even Moses' parents only hid him so long before they entrusted him to a homemade boat on the Nile. Thankfully, God miraculously provided Pharaoh's daughter to find and adopt him, Ex. 2:1-10.

Polygamy is illegal in all Western countries. The problem with bigamy laws is they not only outlaw legally 'marrying' more than one wife, but also outlaw merely 'living as if married' to more than one wife. Also, even if polygyny ever became legal, most local churches would not allow polygynous families to attend, including Abraham's, Moses', and David's if they were here.

Because Bible teachers have been interpreting the Bible according to Roman and Greek culture, instead of according to the text itself, in regards to this issue, for almost two thousand years, even a godly wife will usually think polygamy is sinful, and will not accept a second wife into the family. If you lose your first wife, because you tried to follow the heart of God to never abandon anyone, perhaps after a sin of fornication as referred to Exodus 22:16, then you'll have ended up doing worse than even just following our culture.

It broke Abraham's heart to send Hagar and Ishmael away at the insistence of Sarah; and he would have given them more than bread and a bottle of water if God hadn't assured him of their safety. "The thing was very grievous in Abraham's sight because of his son. And God said unto Abraham, 'Let it not be grievous in your sight because of the lad, and because of your bondwoman. ... Of the son of the bondwoman will I make a nation.' ... And Abraham ... took bread, and a bottle of water, and gave it unto Hagar, putting it on her shoulder, and the child, and sent her away: and she departed, and wandered in the wilderness of Beersheba," Gen. 21:11-14.

Unfortunately, other women aren't guaranteed the miraculous preservation Hagar received, but many may have to be sent away like Hagar because of the heartless world we live in. Only the return of the Lord to establish the Messianic Kingdom can bring relief to all the vulnerable people of this world.

In a perfect world, we wouldn't need polygamy. God's marriage with Israel and Judah occurred because the kingdom split in two after Solomon's reign (though things will still end with God married to both Israel and the church). Jacob's marriage with Leah and Rachel occurred when the wrong bride was slipped into the dark bedroom (which doesn't happen frequently). When fornication occurs, ideally the man would marry the woman even if he's already married, but more ideally, the fornication wouldn't have occurred in the first place.

As I mentioned earlier, I didn't write about polygamy to promote it, but because the cultural perspectives of modern Bible teachers have skewed their interpretations of scripture away from what would otherwise be obvious. Every misinterpretation of scripture causes significant harm to people, and so we need to reconsider this topic today regardless of the risks and difficulties. Teachers that don't understand the biblical definition of adultery allows polygamy can't rightly understand Jesus' teachings on divorce and remarriage, and untold suffering has been inflicted on conscientious believers because of misinterpretations about these issues.

"But speak the things which become sound doctrine: That ... the aged women ... be in behavior as becomes holiness, not false accusers, not given to much wine, teachers of good things. That they may teach the young women to be sober, to love their husbands, to love their children, to be discreet, chaste, keepers at home, good, obedient to their own husbands, that the word of God is not blasphemed. ... For the grace of God that brings salvation has appeared to all men, teaching us that, denying ungodliness and worldly lusts, we should live soberly, righteously, and godly, in this present world; looking for that blessed hope, and the glorious appearing of the great God and our Savior Jesus Messiah; who gave himself for us, that he might redeem us from all iniquity, and purify unto himself a peculiar people, zealous of good works," Titus 2:1-14.

Printed in Great Britain
by Amazon

11052017R00092